TRIAL AND TRIUMPH:
The accounts of Ernie Plantz as
WWII submariner and Japanese P.O.W.

Edited by

Stephen Leal Jackson, Ph.D.

as told by

Ernest V. Plantz

with

Caroline S. Plantz

First published by Dog Ear Publishing
4011 Vincennes Rd
Indianapolis, IN 46268
www.dogearpublishing.net

ISBN: 978-1-4575-4357-9

This book is printed on acid-free paper.

Printed in the United States of America

To the men of the USS *Perch* (SS176),
Good shipmates one and all and especially to
those men who did not survive the Japanese Prison Camp at Makassar.

Charles Newton Brown, MM2 (SS), who died April 18, 1945.

Philip James Dewes, Warrant Officer - Pharmacist, who died July 25,
1945.

Houston Ernest Edwards, EMC (SS) who died July 10, 1944.

Frank Elmer McCreary, MM1 (SS) who died January 4, 1943.

Albert Kenneth Newsome, MMC (SS) who died April 6, 1945.

Robert Archibald Wilson, FC1 (SS) who died June 15, 1945.

Gone from this earth but not forgotten.

TABLE OF CONTENTS

CHAPTER 4.
THE LONG NIGHT BEGINS

CHAPTER 5.
THE DRY SEASON: April to October, 1942

CHAPTER 6.
THE WET SEASON: November 1942 to March 1943

CHAPTER 7.
THE DRY SEASON: April to October, 1943

CHAPTER 8.
THE WET SEASON: November 1943 to March 1944

ACKNOWLEDGEMENTS

IT ALL BEGINS with my family. Isaac Newton's famous quote is so applicable to Sharon; my wife, my friend, and my partner in all things. If I have achieved any measure of success it is because she has helped raise me up to those levels. She has been an unfailing promoter, an insightful critic, and an invaluable supporter. If at times the lines between she and I blur a bit I think that is one of the benefits of spending the better part of a life with the one you were meant for.

My daughter Valerie and my sons Gregory and Alexander also have never been shy about expressing their pride in my writing and research. Whether they know it or not this faith has lifted me during times when the task felt too large or the road too long.

One of the unique resources available to researchers in our geographical area is the Submarine Force Library and Archives, supervised by Archivist Wendy Gully. Ms. Gully was always willing and able to find that one piece of information that otherwise eluded me and for that, and for all of her years of support for the research of the submarine service, she has my gratitude.

Special thanks to Elizabeth P. Sharp for providing excellent and scrupulous editorial assistance. All authors expect to miss a few things when working on a large project. Elizabeth's keen eye and mind found those and an embarrassingly large number of others. This book is much improved by her efforts.

Finally, I would like to acknowledge and express my appreciation for the members of the Eastern USA Chapter U.S. Submarine Veterans of World War II. The constant support and encouragement of these brave men has been a source of strength and an imposition of responsibility to equal the opinion they have of me. My inclusion into their unique brotherhood has been one of the greatest honors I have ever received. I will carry with me always the warmth of their friendship.

ILLUSTRATIONS

Note: Unless otherwise identified, photographs and images are from the personal collection of Ernest V. Plantz

LIST OF ABBREVIATIONS

AS	Auxiliary Ship – Submarine Tender
BB	Battleship
CCC	Civilian Conservation Corps
CO	Commanding Officer
COB	Chief of the Boat
CPO	Chief Petty Officer
DD	Destroyer
EM	Electrician's Mate
EMC	Chief Electrician's Mate
EN	Engineman
ENC	Chief Engineman
F	Fahrenheit
FC	Fire Controlman
FM	Frequency Modulated (Sonar)
LDO	Limited Duty Officer
MM	Machinist's Mate
MMoM	Motor Machinist's Mate
NAVPERS	Naval Personnel Manual
POW	Prisoner of War
RM	Radioman
RMC	Chief Radioman
R&R	Rest and Recreation
SFM	United States Navy Submarine Force Museum
SS	Ship - Submarine
SUBPAC	Commander, Submarine Forces – Pacific Ocean
TDC	Torpedo Data Computer
TM	Torpedoman
USN	United States Navy
USS	United States Ship
XO	Executive Officer

FOREWORD

I FIRST MET Ernest, 'Ernie' Plantz when working on my book, *The Men*. During the course of those interviews, and the interviews that followed for this project, we talked mainly about his time as a prisoner of the Japanese in the POW camp near Makassar on Celebes Island. As they did during all of those afternoons at the Plantz home in Gales Ferry, Connecticut, the voices of Ernie, and his wife Caroline, will lead the reader through his life and experiences with first-person honesty and clarity. Though at times the words are homespun vernacular, they carry the authority of one who has been to and seen a place few on earth can even imagine. It was during one of our sessions at his home that I realized that most of the incidents that he related were either remarkably horrible or extraordinarily humorous. When I mentioned this observation to Ernie he thought for a moment and said, "It seems like when every day is terrible, terrible becomes normal. Only the extra bad and the extra good stand out."

This book, however, is more than a just tale of nearly three and a half years of incarceration, deprivation, and torture. It is about how one man survived that experience and did so while holding true to his conscience, his comrades, and his country; it is a uniquely raw story of an ordinary man who performed an extraordinary feat. The humble and ordinary nature of this patriot only serves to underscore the spirit and resilience of free men who find their best example in Ernie Plantz.

S. L. J., December, 2014

CHAPTER 1

HOW IT ALL BEGAN

His Early Life

Ernie –Age 3

I RETURNED TO the Plantz' home in Gales Ferry, Connecticut in March of 2014 to resume our series of interviews. The day was cold as only a New England spring day can be but the sun shone bright if without much warmth. The interior of their home made up for it though as my arrival was warmly welcomed. Though I felt like a bit of an intruder Ernie and Caroline soon brought me into their circle and made me feel like a regular and valued guest. Lots of folks like to talk to Ernie and mostly they want to hear about his time in the

Imperial Japanese POW camp and certainly that is especially interesting. However, in order to understand how a person reacts when placed in an incredible experience like that I thought it was important to understand the foundation on which that later person was built. So, we began his story at his own beginning.

Steve:	Okay. Let's get started. You remember my digital recorder? I'm going to move this closer to the center there so it should get everything.
Ernie:	He's got a little thing on the recorder that cuts the wife out if she talks too much.
Caroline:	Ernie!
Steve:	No, no, I leave it all in; it's all valuable. Okay, so we are going to start right back at the beginning of the Ernie story; back to when and where you were born. And let's see what I had. I had that you were born in Spring Hill, West Virginia.
Ernie:	Yeah. That later became South Charleston, but it was Spring Hill at that point in time. I had a brother and two sisters; I was the oldest. Clifford, he was born just after me, then two younger sisters; Garnet and Norma Lee; Garnet was the young devil.

Norma – 1940 – Age 11

2

Norma Lee was the angel; she could do no wrong. Norma was born when I was eight. I was sent to get the midwife late at night and I had to walk by the cemetery. I whistled all the way; they didn't get me!

She graduated from high school in 1946. I'm lucky I have a picture of her. We didn't take many pictures back then. It cost money.

Caroline: And his mother was Nancy Hill Plantz, I don't think we gave you the "Hill." She was one, Steve, who only saw the good in people . There was never any bad; she always saw the positive. She didn't know how to read very well; she had only gone as far as first grade in school, but she couldn't go to the bathroom without her Bible. Oh, she was wonderful and she never missed a Sunday at church. Grandpa took her but he never went in, but he always took her. He went to church four times on a Sunday; he took her there, dropped her off, went back, picked her up, took her back again at night, went back, picked her up again but never went inside.

Ernie's mother was a sweetheart.

Ernie: Yup. A little country girl.

Caroline: She was a prize. She was a fun one. Such a good cook.

Ernie: She was a good one.

Caroline: Every time I went to her house, I gained ten pounds. I got to the point of saying, I can't go again because I never lost the weight. First time we took my mother there for breakfast she said, "What is this? Thanksgiving dinner?"

She was the best cook ever. She was here one time and I tried to learn how to make her biscuits because she made the best biscuits ever. She never measured anything. She'd grab the next ingredient and I'd say "Okay mom, wait, let me see how much that is." But she'd just move on to the next step and I'd say, "Wait mom, don't put it in yet; I've got to measure!" Not her, though; she never measured.

3

Steve: She sounds like she was what we imagine a real country woman to be like; she was a great cook and had a deep religious faith and though she had little schooling she had a big heart. How about your father Ernie?

Ernie: My father's name was Everett Ellsworth Plantz. He was a lead burner helper at the nearby Union Carbide Plant. Part of his job required him to unroll huge rolls of lead with only brute force. Yeah, you'd brace your back against the wall and then your heels would begin to roll the lead and let it push that way to roll it.

One day, when I was just three years old, he was pushing on one of these rolls of lead and something in his back popped and some part of his skeletal structure became misaligned. And, you know, one leg became shorter than the other. That's the truth. He could no longer work at his job and remained disabled for most of his adult life.

I think that every spare dollar that the family had went to take him everywhere that he heard that someone was working miracles with disabled folks. After the accident he never walked more than five-hundred feet without setting down on a cushion and resting to get the weight off of that leg. Finally around the late 1970s while visiting Norma in Arizona he found a chiropractor that cured him. He did adjustments, of course, but also made him walk around barefoot all the time. When he started one of my Dad's legs was almost an inch shorter than the other; don't you know when he was done they were the same length. Cured him. He became quite a walker after that.

Steve: That accident must have had quite an impact on your family.

Ernie: It did indeed. When Dad got crippled my grandmother was coming down with cancers of the stomach, they made a deal with Mom; if she would take care of Grandma, then we could move in with them and farm. So my mom essentially became a housewife for two families and we had a nice place to live. My dad was ill. He couldn't work almost at all.

The farm was a good place to live but it was a spare, hard living. My whole wardrobe was two shirts, two pair of pants, and one pair of shoes. We had no electricity, no running water, and no toilet inside just a two-holer outhouse. But we managed to stay clean somehow, some way, and all-in-all it was a nice life.

Steve: So you all moved onto your grandfather Plantz's farm. What was he like?

Ernie: Jacob Maxwell Plantz; he was always called just J. M. Didn't like the name Jacob. He was there all the time I was growing up and I worked side-by-side with him on the farm. When I wasn't in school I was working with Grandpa. He was quite a character really. He didn't drink and he didn't smoke and he just worked. You could almost say he worked from daylight to dark. He would get up at 4:30 in the morning, as soon as the first crack of light, and build the fire in the cookstove. Get it hot and ready to go and then he'd wake my Mom and get her up to make biscuits. So her day started in by probably five o'clock or somewhere along there. Much earlier than she had to get up."

Steve: I'll bet your Mom's good cooking put some weight on him.

Ernie: Oh no, he was thin as a rail. Here he is with his second wife some time later on. I don't remember her name. They were in Florida although he still kept his West Virginia look.

He never weighed more than a hundred and fifteen pounds in his life, and yet he ate all these things that make people fat. He loved sweets. He lived on them. Sweets and homemade biscuits and any fat he could get a hold of. He didn't ever gain weight. All his life he was that way.

Caroline:	How tall a person was he?
Ernie:	I would say probably five foot ten. Like a beanpole.
Ernie:	When I was older I asked my grandfather J.M. a man to man question. I asked him, I said "Grandpa, how old does a man have to be before he's too old to...." J.M. was 86 at the time. He answered, "I don't know, son, you'll have to talk to a man older than I am."
Steve:	He sounds like a kindly man with an appreciation for humor but there must have been lots of opportunities for mischief on the farm. Did you ever get him mad at you?
Ernie:	Oh, certainly. When I wasn't in the field with him, I was tinkering with farm equipment or something like that. I remember one time, I did what I call a clincher. There's the bead that goes around the old automobile tire and they would cut it off to make a boot out of the tire to go in a bad spot. I picked that thing up, and of course it was wiry and course, and I whacked

Grandpa in the legs with it. He took it away from me and beat the hell out of me with it.

Another time, a couple of cousins and I, we got up on top of this damn flat-roofed garage. I was up there with my brother and we had a four-wheel toy fire wagon up there. My brother wanted to ride it but I was in it so he tried to push me over the side in that damn thing. He was trying to kill me and he damn near succeeded. Dog-gone wagon had one wheel where the rubber tire was gone, so every time you went around on the roof, it cut the roof. Grandpa got after us for that one, and he gave us a good licking. Those were the only times I ever remember he really got mad with me and, as you can see, I deserved it.

Steve: So you had a few interesting farm adventures.

Ernie: Always. I remember I was probably ten or eleven years old when my sister Garnet dropped a hatchet on my foot. I say dropped but she was fooling around pretending to chop my foot and then actually did, that devil. My sis was six and I was four years older than her. She got a good spanking from our mother for cracking my foot. My mom poured salt in that wound and then poured turpentine on it and wrapped it up and it didn't get infected a darn bit; it just healed right up. Salt and turpentine: poor-folk medicine.

Steve: You did say turpentine, right?

Ernie: Yes. It sounds wrong but it did right. I wouldn't do it now but it worked fine back then.

Caroline: She sure was a wonder. But, J. M.? Well I never knew him but I know that J. M. was his idol.

Steve: What about the other side of the family? Was it Hill?

Caroline: Then the other grandfather, he was Big Foot, right?

Ernie: He was Big Foot, yeah. Here he is wrangling a couple of horses.

Caroline:	Joe Hill was his name.
Ernie:	Joe Hill, uh huh.
Caroline:	Now what was Joe Hill like?
Ernie:	He was kind of a quiet guy. Yeah. He was a trader basically. He had the knack. Always seemed to get the best of whomever he was dealing with. It was like he could start with a broken clasp knife and end up with an automobile. That was Grandpa Hill.

This here is Grandpa and Grandma Hill. I don't know what they're up to but there they are. Occasionally, I'd go across the hill to his place and spend the night there. They always had fruit from their farm and lots of good things to eat. In the morning then I'd go back home. You walked; you didn't have any conveyance to ride. We had an old car, but you didn't start it up to ride five miles. You walked.

Steve: So you did have a car though?

Ernie: We had a big flat bed truck that was the farm truck. I don't know how many pounds that thing would hall, but it was a lot. It had a magneto start, no battery, you ran off the magneto and sometimes you had to really crank to start it; that crank would be stiff and hard to turn. So we used to park it on the hill above the barn so that you could start it down a hill and let it coast on its own to start it. It was a beautiful running machine.

We would use it on big trips to town and such. We lived about a mile from a concrete hardtop roadway but the road to it was dirt. In the winter time that dirt road would get so soft that the car would bury up to the axels in the mud. So we'd take our horses and hitch them to the truck and the horses would drag it to the hardtop. We'd ride the truck into town and when we came back, Grandpa would be waiting with the horses again to drag us back home. That was one of our lesser fun things, the horses pulling that truck so we didn't make that trip except for important reasons.

One of those was to shop for the food we couldn't grow or make on the farm. We used to shop on Saturday night at the food store because at the end of the week usually bananas were marked down to a cent a pound. They didn't have refrigeration and they couldn't keep them over the weekend so they would sell them for a cent a pound just to get rid of them. We waited until just about closing time to buy these bananas and when we got them home and we'd take some of them and make banana ice cream. Some of them went for just regular eating.

Steve: Tell me a little about Grandma Hill.

Ernie: I don't remember much about Sally - Grandma Hill. All I remember about her is that she was a good cook. She made buttermilk biscuits which were just as good as or better than my Mom's and that's saying something. Always made a white gravy in the morning.

She also had a jar in her kitchen that had this mixture in it, and I questioned her one morning. I said, "Grandma, what is that?" She said, "Oh, that's crazy tonic. It makes you feel good. You want some of it?" I said, sure. So she gave me a glass of this stuff and I swallowed it, and it was Epsom salts and lemon juice with a little sugar added. I went like going over the moon. I lived in the outhouse for a while after that. And that's about all that I remember about her.

Steve: That was a harsh lesson! Maybe she had a bit of a sense of humor.

Okay. Let's talk a little bit about your life away from the farm. What was school like for you during those days?

Ernie: Mr. Lily was my grade school teacher. It was a one-room schoolhouse and he had from third to the eighth grade in one room and he taught us all. I learned a lot that way by listening to what was going on with the older kids. He scaled the questions to what he knew your grade level was. He was pretty darn good at it, really.

If you screwed it up or talked when you weren't supposed to or something, he had a heavy-duty fountain pen. He used to rub that thing on the back of your neck. Boy, did it hurt like heck. It wouldn't leave any marks, but it sure hurt when he ruffled those hairs. You didn't talk too much out of turn after he did that. He was good. He was a good teacher. I learned a lot from him. He could be a nice guy too. At Christmas time, he used to buy each one of the kids a pound of candy, chocolate-coated cherries candies. They're good stuff. I can still taste them today. That was about thirty-three kids. Out of a year's salary of his, why it took a good chunk of it. Back then, he only got about $400 a year for teaching. You figure you buy that many candies, that was pretty generous.

Steve: Did you go home for lunch or did you bring your own?

Ernie: I used to take onions to school for lunch. Well, actually, along the road I'd pull up wild onions and put a bunch of them in my lunch pail. We used to have a Burnside stove in the classroom that had a rim that went around the top, a flat rim, that fit on the stove pipe. If we had a fire going in the stove, that rim would get hot along with the stove. Those of us that had leftover home-cooked meals for lunch would put their lunch pails on the rim and their lunch would get hot. Since mine had these wild onions in the pail pretty soon when they'd start getting hot and they'd practically run us out of the room they'd get so strong smelling. The teacher didn't like that at all.

I always had to take biscuits because we didn't have any other kind of bread and I was kind of ashamed to because it seemed like poor food. But the doggone kids that went to school with me loved those biscuits! I saw them as plain food, they saw them as treats. They'd trade me their light-bread sandwiches for my biscuits so I did all right.

Steve: Seems like the farm produced pretty well for your family.

Ernie: That's not all we produced! J. M. and my father also had a good moonshine business going. My grandfather did all of the heavy work and my father tended the still. Not much moving for that so he could just lie there and make sure it was working right.

Steve: So they made moonshine?

11

Ernie: That's right. Of course it was illegal so we had to hide what we were doing although it was probably no great secret. When J. M. would set out a barrel of mash for fermentation he would take that damn barrel which weighed probably fifty, sixty pounds itself and put fifty pounds of cracked corn in it, seventy-five pounds of sugar in it and carry it into the woods. I don't know how in the hell he did it! Like I said he didn't weigh over one hundred and fifteen pounds. He was strong as a mule. And after he got the barrels of mash then he'd have to carry the water and that's damn heavy too. They would always run the still at night. It would be daylight when they set it up but they always used the distillery at night and then only when they had dried locust wood that they used to feed the fire. It burned nice without a lot of smoke. Dad used that forever.

Steve: That's amazing. How did they sell the moonshine?

Ernie: My father used to deliver milk in bulk form. He could sit to drive and walk short distances but with pain. He had regular customers for the milk and some for the moonshine too. I know one of his stops in town was at the district court and also to somebody in the sheriff's department.

Steve: How did he do that? Did he sneak the bottles into those places?

Ernie: No sneaking. He would go right up the courthouse steps with his stuff right out in the open because the jug of whiskey was painted white and the people thought it was milk, but no: he delivered one gallon of milk and one gallon of whiskey. He took them right up the courthouse steps to the judge. Yeah, went right up the courthouse steps with his stuff right out in the open with that jug of whiskey painted white.

Steve: So the people who worked in the courthouse were buying it?

Ernie: Oh, yeah! Oh, yeah. Even the judge was buying it; the same guy that's going to sentence you for moonshining when you come up on the docket.

Steve: So the good product wouldn't buy you any leniency?

Ernie: Nope. And we found that out because the good times came to an end one day. I guess I was senior in high school and the cops spotted the still and they waited until Dad showed up and got the thing going. I was walking down the doggone hill near the barbwire fence to go see my Dad and this doggone cop jumps up like out of the ground hollering with his gun drawn. He was hollering and I took off at high speed, down the hill, jumped the barbwire fence right where the cop was at and ran down to the still where Dad was. I ran past Dad hollering myself, "Cops! Cops!" and continued back around to the farmhouse. I guess I knew what was coming and didn't see any purpose for me getting arrested. Of course Dad was crippled and couldn't run but he knew what was up. By the time they got Dad collected and brought up to the house, hell I was in the house studying like I'd been sitting there for hours; I didn't say a word.

They talked the officer into taking my grandpa to jail because Dad was crippled. Dad agreed to come the next day to be locked up, so that's the way it worked. They took Grandpa, who was innocent as a newborn child, took him into the courthouse and locked him up for the night. And Dad surrendered the next morning so they turned Grandpa loose and locked Dad up. He pled guilty and was given probation. It was a given fact that back in those days that most families knew how to make corn whiskey and at different times they all made corn whiskey. They didn't look on themselves as lawbreakers but them damn federal people did. That was when he got arrested. It was 1939. Anyway, that was my introduction to the law.

13

Working in the CCC

The Civilian Conservation Corps (CCC) was a public work relief program that was created as part of the New Deal to provide employment for young men during the Great Depression. The CCC's mission was to conserve, restore, and develop land in rural areas controlled by federal and state agencies. Parks, trails, and other natural recreational areas were developed while providing a structured and meaningful work experience for unemployed men. The quasi-military structure of the Corps provided the means to develop morale and stamina in these men and may have indirectly created a ready-made military savvy force in advance of the huge personnel build-up that the World War would soon necessitate. At its height the CCC employed nearly 300,000 men.[1]

Steve:	We've got a page here from your high school yearbook, I guess.
Ernie:	Yes. That's it; old South Charleston High.
Steve:	You don't say too much about your high school experience.
Ernie:	Well, I went and I did okay, but my focus was on the farm. I always wanted to do things and not talk about doing things. But I did it because I knew it had to be done. And there's the evidence right on the page, me, on the bottom again.
Steve:	Maybe that's a foreshadowing of your submarine career!
Ernie:	Ha! Could be, could be. Anyway you can see I wasn't much of a joiner, so to speak. I had plenty of things to occupy my time around the farm. But I did like to read; always have.
Ernie:	Well anyway, I graduated from high school in 1939. So I had a diploma but what was I going to do with it? There was no work except the farm work, and that was a dollar a day, if you could get it. Of course I still worked on our farm but I got no money for that. I wanted money but more than that, I wanted a career. I'd been doing farm work for years and years and I was hungry for something more. Opportunities were very slim but I decided to join the CCC and see where that took me.

14

Stephen Leal Jackson

HARRY D. DUDLEY
"Newt"
Musical

Band .... '33, '37
Aviation Club .... '33, '34

RUTH LOUISE FOWLKES
"Woofie"
Popular

Pres. Home Room .... '35
"Seventeen" .... '36
Pres. Travel Club .... '36
Drum Majorette .... '35, '37
Dramatic Club .... '36, '37
Sec. Dram. .... '37, '38
X-Ray Staff .... '38, '39
"The Right Answer" .... '38
State Band Festival ...... '36, '38

JACK P. DRIGGS
"Skinny"
Dependable

Aviation Club .... '35, '36
Outdoor Club .... '36, '37

MARY FRANCES SMITH
"Doddu"
Precocious

Marionette Club .... '34
French Club .... '36
Organizer of History Club ... '38
Glee Club .... '39
Chairman Decorating Comm.
    for Commencement Ex. ... '38
Pres. of Home Room ..... '34, '35
Knitting Club .... '37

ERNEST PLANTZ
"Ernie"
Modest

Reading Club .... '35, '39

VIRGINIA DARE HUTCHINSON
"Jinny"
Subdued

Charm Club .... '35
Girl Reserves .... '37, '38

ROBERT B. CLAY
"Bob"
Agreeable

Reading Club .... '34, '36
Scout Club .... '36, '37
Chess and Checker Club. '37, '39
Sec. and Treas. Home
    Room .... '38, '39
Football .... '37, '38
Basketball .... '36, '39

STELLA MAY LEWIS
"Prize Fighter"
Sport

Outdoor Club .... '35
Sewing Club .... '36
Cooking Club .... '37
Swing Club .... '38

PAUL SULLIVAN
"Sully"
Contemplative

Aviation .... '35, '37
Chess and Checker .... '37, '39
Basketball .... '35, '39

ETHEL FAIRE HAYNES
"Effie"
Peppy

Girls' Basketball .... '36
Knitting Club .... '36
Game Club .... '36, '37
Marionette Club .... '34, '36
Movie Appreciation .... '38

PAGE TWENTY-TWO

South Charleston High School Yearbook, 1939

15

Steve:	The Civilian Conservation Corps?
Ernie:	That's right. After I graduated high school in '39, I went into the CCC; Davis Creek Camp company 2599, and I was in there from late summer '39 to about July of '40. It wasn't the best but it was something different. Also, by joining the CCCs I got twenty dollars a month; that was cash-money which was rare enough at that time. I got five and my mom got the rest; they sent the fifteen dollars directly to the family. It really was a good program I think. Took idle young men, taught them to do some hard work and work together, put a little money in their pockets and helped out the families back home. I liked it; I was hungry for work.
Steve:	Now how far away was the CCC camp?
Ernie:	Well, it was about, probably seven miles from where I lived. From town it was probably another five or six. It was just across the hills. I say I "went into" the CCC but it was more like enlisting. You had to sign up for a year and the organization was quite military. We had uniforms and ranks, people in charge and all kinds of military procedure. It was organized just like an Army company I imagine. Here is a picture of morning colors which sort of gives you a feeling of our military styles.

Ernie: You can see part of our company standing in formation in our uniforms. There were about two-hundred of us recruits. The little signal cannon has just been fired. Very military.

You can just see the barracks in the background. There were fifty of us to a barrack. Some CCC companies had only tents, but we had wooden barrack buildings so I guess we were lucky in that way. Here is a better picture of them and the whole company.

Ernie: A little crooked on the camera work but it gives you the idea. Regular military rules. We were all young, energetic men; we needed it I think. It was not a bad place to be and it helped out the family.

Steve: What kind of work did they have you do there?

Ernie: The work that we did was fighting forest fires in our district. When we weren't fighting forest fires we were making a state park that included building a dam across the stream, which was probably fifty foot wide. We had to shape the forms and build that dam by wheelbarrow and cement; dumping it in all by hand. Once you started pouring that cement, you had to keep pouring because it was a day and night project keeping it from setting up on you. So, we built a dam across that stream and then diverted the water back around it. That was day and night pace until that was all good. My job was that I either loaded baskets or crushed rock; preferred the crushed rock job. We also built lots of things over time. Some small road work, cutting trails through the state park, and generally clearing out the underbrush. All by hand too; there were plenty of us strong young men so no need for any machinery!

Steve: Fire fighting, dam building, road and trail building, and general construction; that sounds like a lot of work.

Ernie: It was, but there was time for recreation as well. They had a well-equipped woodworking shop that we could use when our work was done or on weekends.

Steve: Was it just there for your recreation?

Ernie: No. Certain men worked there during the day making signs and furniture and such as that for the state park; picnic tables, benches, guardrails, trail markers and all manner of wooden things. Only when the shop was idle could we use it and I did.

Steve: Did you make anything special?

Ernie: Well, we had a neighbor back home that had some black walnut on her property and I got a piece of that. I took that wood to a sawmill in town and had it planed down both sides and cut to the length I wanted. I traded about half the wood I brought to the sawmill for the work they did. That was beautiful wood.

Steve: Black walnut; that is some nice wood!

Ernie: Yes it was. So I took it on the bus back to the CCC camp. When I had the time I made a magazine book rack out of it and a lamp. The lamp's there next to you but my magazine rack got burned when the farm house burned down many years later. The lamp is still in good shape, though.

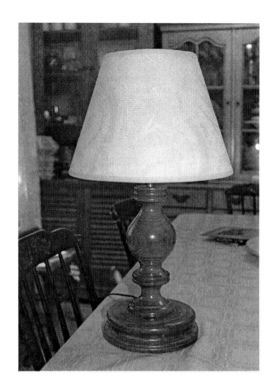

Steve:	It does NOT look seventy-five years old!
Ernie:	I rubbed that wood with linseed oil, that's the trick.
Steve:	Beautiful workmanship. Now you left all that good food and that good cooking back on the farm. How was the food at the CCC camp?
Ernie:	Regular army food. I do remember the spaghetti and meat; that wasn't bad at all and it was new to me. To this day I still like spaghetti and meat; not meatballs, more like meat sauce I guess you'd say. That's what we had there. I can't remember what we ate for breakfast. It mustn't have been too special.
	I was there for almost a year so I got to experience winter in the barracks; made you long for summer. This picture gives you a little idea of how cold it got.

Ernie:	You can see those icicles and the stove chimneys so you know where most of the heat was going. But we were young and tough and we all survived.
Steve:	Sounds like it was mostly work though.
Ernie:	That is true but there was time for things like my wood project and some sports. There were always the typical bull-sessions and some ball games. Occasionally the Tobacco Deer would visit.
Steve:	I'm sorry, what was that?
Ernie:	Tobacco Deer we called it. It was a regular wild deer that would come into camp and became almost tame. I imagine at first it picked up cigarette butts and got a taste for them somehow. Anyway, after a while if you held up a part of a cigarette that critter would walk up to you and eat it right out of your hand. It was the darnedest thing; the Tobacco Deer. Not skittish in the least; even posed for pictures:

Ernie: Here's the Tobacco Deer with our top sergeant...

Ernie: ...and here he is with the Camp Commandant. Isn't that the darnedest thing? It's doing a trick for a little tobacco. I don't know what the attraction was for that animal.

Steve: How long were you in the CCC?

Ernie: Well, you had to sign-up for a year and I signed-up in September of 1939. I should have stayed until September, 1940 but I got out early.

Steve: Why was that?

Ernie: They would let you out if you joined one of the branches of the military, and that's what I did. I joined the navy.

Chapter 1 Notes:

1.   http://www.ccclegacy.org/CCC_Brief_History.html   [accessed 1/5/2015].

CHAPTER 2

FROM CIVILIAN TO SAILOR

Ernie Joins the Navy

IN JULY OF 1940 the United States was still at peace but a large portion of the rest of the world was at war. Japan and China were engaged in what was called the Second Sino-Japanese War. The Nanking Massacre and the bombing of the U. S. Navy river gunboat USS *Panay* (PR-5) both occurred in December, 1937. This war continued until it was enveloped into the greater conflict in December, 1941.

The summer of 1940 also saw a Europe vastly changed from even a year earlier. Nazi Germany ceased its non-aggressive expansion and invaded and occupied Poland in September, 1939. Norway fell to the Nazis in April of 1940 and Germany invaded Belgium, France, Luxembourg and the Netherlands in May; France officially surrendered to the Nazis on June 25th. The air war against Great Britain, known as the Battle of Britain, began on July 10th; this was to be a preamble to the planned Nazi invasion of the United Kingdom, Operation Sea Lion. This was the state of the world as Ernie entered the Navy.

Steve: You enlisted the 20th of July, 1940.

Ernie: Yep; enlisted at Charleston, West Virginia recruiting station.

Steve: Why did you decide do that?

Ernie: Well, I had a cousin that was in the navy. Harold Costa. He was a Radioman First Class and he was telling me how good the food was and it was a great place to learn a trade. He was in submarines also and

I talked to him and he convinced me that submarines was the way to go because you got treated better, you ate better, and you got more pay. You got more pay! That was an extra incentive. You got $10 more a month for being on the submarines. And I wanted to be an electrician, so up there was where I enlisted in the navy and I had a better chance at being an electrician so I did. My parents were poor. I had no opportunity to go to college. And so the navy seemed like a good spot for me. They paid twenty-one dollars a month. That was apprentice seaman wages. Here's me and little Garnet.

September 1940
Ernest Plantz brother
Garnet Plantz and sister

Steve:	Where did you go to boot camp?
Ernie:	Oh, Norfolk, Virginia. U S of A. July '40 to October '40 was at USNTC, Norfolk. United States Naval Training Center.
Steve:	Okay. And then after boot camp?
Ernie:	Yeah, when I graduated from boot camp, I went home on 30 days leave and then I reported aboard the battleship *New Mexico* in San Diego.
Steve:	How did you get to San Diego?
Ernie:	How did I get to San Diego? By train.
Steve:	Cross country?
Ernie:	Right. Once I got on we went to the Navy Yard over in Washington State and then back to San Diego and then immediately to Pearl.
Steve:	Pearl, okay. Good. San Diego, Bremerton, San Diego, Pearl. Good.
Ernie:	Actually we went from the shipyard to San Francisco to take on ammunition and then we went to San Diego, only for a short time, and then Hawaii.
Steve:	So you were on the USS *New Mexico* (BB-40) from October 1940 to April 1941 stationed at Pearl Harbor. How did you like that?
Ernie:	I didn't.
Caroline:	Why not?
Ernie:	Well, they wanted me to be on the deck-force and I just wanted to be an electrician. So, they wouldn't let me go in the black deck. In that day they had the black deck and the white deck. Topside people were white and below decks were black.
Steve:	You wanted to be an electrician pretty bad.
Ernie:	Well I was attracted to the work of the electricians. I knew civilian electricians were always employed, and envied the electricians on the battleship. Most of them ran around changing light bulbs. I used to watch these electricians run around in clean dungarees changing light bulbs in envy, you know?

Steve: Was that your only disappointment with life on the battleship?

Ernie: No. The food wasn't very good, it wasn't very plentiful. I, being one of the junior members of the crew, the way they arranged it, as a way of training you I guess, was you were seated at a table with a petty officer first class in charge of the table, and second class, and third class, and leading seamen, and then the most junior person sat at the far end of the table. Well the mess cook went to the galley to get the food, they carried it back to the berthing space because that's where you ate. Then it started at the head of the table. The first class, they took what they wanted. It went down the line by the rates. When it got down to me, often times the tureen was empty. So the cook had to rush back to the galley to see if he could get seconds. And if he did, instead of starting where they left off so I could get food, they started again at the head of the table. And sometimes on seconds I didn't get any either. And so it was; I wasn't happy.

Steve: That's got to have been frustrating.

Ernie: It was. When we got to Pearl Harbor I made another appeal for a transfer to Engineering and the Electrician's Mate rating. I was again refused. Then I got a dinner invitation that changed the course of my life. A friend of mine from back home, Harold Raybel, invited me over to his submarine, the *Plunger*, which was stationed in Pearl, to have dinner with him. After that one dinner on that submarine I said, "Man, this is the place for me."

Caroline: Yea, but how'd you get off the *New Mexico*?

Ernie: Well the Navy asked for volunteers for Asiatic station. They sent a squadron of subs out there. I think it was August [1940], they sent another squadron of submarines to Manila. They had to know something was coming. So, I volunteered for the group. That's when I had to go see the Executive Officer on the battleship and get permission to put in a request. Well, I put in the first of two transfer requests. The first one went to my Division Officer and he disapproved. So, the second one went to the Executive Officer direct because my Division Officer said if it got disapproved it could go direct to XO. So, I put another one in to the XO and with a note to why I wanted to leave. I got called up to his stateroom. And he looks up and says, "You want to go to the Asiatic Station son?" I said, "Yes sir." He says. "Well, have your things ready. Be ready to go at seven o'clock tomorrow morning." And he says, "The group will be forming up and you'll be on your way." I says "Thank you sir." That's how I got selected. When it came time to go the XO was on deck. He wouldn't even shake hands with me. I do remember that the lieutenant, my division officer, wished me good luck grudgingly before I left.

It was April of 1941 when Ernie volunteered for submarine duty in the Asiatic Station. At that time, the war in Europe was over a year old and tensions were continuing to heat up in the Japanese sphere of influence. The United States was increasing its military presence in the Far East and this meant, among other things, adding another submarine squadron to the Asiatic Fleet stationed in Manila, Philippines. Ernie was assigned to the USS *Perch* (SS 176), a *Porpoise* Class fleet submarine stationed in Manila as a "direct input"; he was not required to first attend Sub School. He felt that this normal prerequisite was not required "…because they were desperate for people for submarines out on the old China Station in the Philippines." Ernie had escaped the rigid formality of the battleship and was headed to the easy camaraderie of the submarine fleet.

From Surface to Submarine: Transfer to the Silent Service

The USS *Perch* (SS 176), was a *Porpoise* Class submarine of the P-5 subclass. The *Perch* was built at the Electric Boat shipyard and launched in 1936. This boat had welded hull construction unlike several other boats in the same class which had the older style riveted hulls. While the *Perch* and her sister submarines had many improvements from previous classes they were still not quite "fleet" boats, this is able to equal the speed, range, and relative firepower of the surface fleet components. This was mainly due to her insufficient top speed as her range and weaponry rivaled the later "true" fleet boats. The next class of submarines, the *Salmon* class, would become the first U. S. submarine to achieve the twenty-one knot top surfaced speeds that allowed them to operate with the battleships of the surface fleet

Photo # NH 42897   USS Perch in harbor, circa 1936-1937

Perch (SS-176), in a harbor, circa 1936-1937.
USN photo # NH 42897, from the collections of the
US Naval Historical Center.

Steve: So how did you get from Pearl Harbor to Manila?

Ernie: I left Pearl in April 1941 and went to Manila on the old transport ship USS *Henderson*. She was like a bus and made a regular loop around the Pacific picking up and dropping off folks. San Francisco, Pearl, and Manila; sometimes Shanghai too I think. Just round and round its route just like a bus route. The transport *Chaumont* did much the same but tended to stop at Shanghai more often till that city was lost.

Steve: Okay. So you got to Manila and reported to the *Perch*.

Ernie: Not immediately. I had diarrhea on the *Henderson* and a high fever; might have been a touch of dysentery. I think that affected my memory. They sent me to a receiving station until I was well enough to report. Then I went onto the *Perch*.

Steve: Now you wanted to be an Electrician but was that assured for you?

Ernie: Not at all. I had to strike for it. But I went for it right away. I checked aboard the submarine and of course the COB is the first authority that you meet. He talked to me and wanted to know what I wanted to strike for. I told him I wanted to strike for Electrician. He said, well he says, "Well I'll talk to the Engineer." And he did and the Engineer cornered me then in the Control Room, introduced himself and said, "I hear you want to be an Electrician." I said, "Yes sir." He says "Well," he says, "Are you a high school graduate?" And I said, "Yes sir." And then he says to me "Well" he says, "Do you drink?" I didn't quite know how to answer him. I says, "Yes sir, but I'm not very good at it." I says, "I'm getting better!" He looked at me just casually and said, "You'll do." That's how I got started being qualified to be an Electrician.

Steve: Electrician striker? Sounds more like a drinker striker.

Ernie: Yes, yes! There was plenty of that.

Steve: When did they start calling you, "The Kid?"

29

Ernie:	Almost soon as I reported on *Perch*. I was the youngest one they put on board, so I was automatically, The Kid. The name stuck. I was sort of a bashful fellow, not too prone to speak up.
Steve:	Did you have a baby face?
Ernie:	Yeah. Not much whiskers, so they called me The Kid.
Steve:	Now what kind of things did they have you do when you first reported aboard?
Ernie:	Well, mess cooking of course. Every new guy had to do that. But mess cooking, if you used your time, you had a lot of time when you weren't doing mess cooking duties. So after the meal when you'd cleaned up, well, you had time and if you were mess cooking you didn't have to stand any other watches. So I used the time to trace systems and make my drawings and get my notebook ready so I could qualify.
Steve:	Did you start working with the electricians?
Ernie:	Well, like I said I became an Electrician Striker. But mess cooking and qualifying in subs; those were my main jobs. So, that's what I did, during my first three months time. I had more time than I'd ever had to myself, so I studied and found all those who would give a system checkout and got my booklet signed off early. Once I did all the system drawings I was virtually ready to get qualified. I had memorized all that stuff that you had to do. They thought that I was pretty keen since I did it so fast. I qualified [in submarines] in July of '41.
Steve:	Yeah, that's quick.
Ernie:	Yeah. I was in a hurry. I told them, "I'm in a hurry" and I was. I guess I wanted to get going with life. My *New Mexico* time was like just standing still.
Steve:	I see. You arrived on the *Perch* in April of 1941. What was duty in the Philippines like before the war started? What kind of things did the *Perch* do? Were they just anchored all the time? Did they go out?

30

Ernie: They did operations on a weekly basis. Mostly it was down in the Celebes Sea, down near Borneo we practiced firing torpedoes, training drills, and then we would come back to Manila at the end of the week or we went to one of the other islands for a weekend and back to Manila. We were also continually practicing our battle drills like shooting torpedoes, making runs on targets and practicing crash dives. Lots of practice and operations in the local area around Manila. We also practiced with destroyers; they would make a run on us and we would try and evade. We did a lot of that during that time period. We were pretty good; they never did detect us, which was bad I think.

During this time I was also busy learning my job as an Electrician and qualifying as lookout when surfaced, and at the bow and stern planes station when submerged. As an Electrician striker I did a little bit of everything: watering the batteries, taking gravities on the batteries, repairing electrical equipment, or just changing light bulbs. It seems from the time I was aboard until the war started when the Japs bombed Pearl Harbor we trained weekly, sometimes monthly and ran around the Philippines.

Steve: At the time did you think you were preparing for war?

Ernie: No. We could read newspapers so we knew the state of things. I don't think I saw anything unusual in all our practice. That is sort of what warships do; practice, practice. Looking back I can see that maybe we were preparing more than normal; however, at the time it seemed routine. I still had plenty of time to get into trouble.

Steve: How's that?

Ernie: We were in Mariveles Shipyard side by side with the USS *Porpoise*. They got tied up outboard in our area in the shipyard. We all went to shore together and we ended up in the same bar. I had a big fight with a *Porpoise* sailor named Lacy, a torpedo man from their forward room. Not a bad guy just got my blood up. I don't know what started it but I accused him of stealing our electric gear. We got into a battle. I knocked him down and out and went back to my drinking. Pretty soon he tapped me on the shoulder and wanted to know if I was the guy that hit him. I said "Yeah, you want some more?" He says "Yeah; let's go outside and finish it." We went outside and he knocked me down, I knocked him down. It was a pretty good mess because it was muddy outside. We were a sight to behold; muddy, bloody, black and blue. Anyway, the guys got me out of there and back on board and put a big fat steak on my eye because I had a massive black eye. Put a steak on it! The next morning the skipper called me in and said "Heard you had a little problem in Mariveles last night." I said yeah I did. He said "Well, what happened?" I said well I don't remember exactly now what he said but it was something bad about my crew so I invited him for a little battle outside and he accepted. I said this is what I got as a result of that battle. He says that the skipper of the *Porpoise* reported it and I talked to him and he's very upset. My captain said "I'm going to have to do something." My chin dropped when he said "When we leave here, I've got to hold mast on you." I guess he saw that I was a little bit dejected about it because he said "Don't worry. We're getting underway for Manila this afternoon. It'll be regular liberty in Manila. There's no more liberty here for you but we're getting underway soon." I felt better after that one.

Caroline: Terrible punishment for you.

Ernie: That's the best fight I've ever had anywhere. It was that one.

Caroline: I believe it.

CHAPTER 3

ERNIE AND THE PERCH GO TO WAR

Manila Under Attack

THE UNITED STATES maintained components of its naval forces in what was called the Asiatic Fleet. These various ships were stationed in various places in China and the Philippines including Manila Bay and the nearby Mariveles Shipyard. At the onset of World War Two twenty-nine submarines were members of the Asiatic Fleet. These mostly consisted of older class boats of the *Porpoise* and *Salmon* classes and even several of the S-boats built between 1918 and 1925. A number of these boats were on the scene in Manila Bay when the Japanese attacked the islands.

Steve: Now where were you when the war began?

Ernie: Ringside. The *Perch* was anchored out in Manila Bay on December 8th; that was their Pearl Harbor Day.

Steve: Ringside? Tell me more about that.

Ernie: The *Perch* was anchored in Manila Bay because they didn't have much pier service so you anchored along-side the tender or you anchored in the middle of the bay. We were anchored in the bay undergoing a two-week upkeep. And we had the old Winton two-cycle diesel engines which were terrible oil leakers and required a lot of extra maintenance. It was almost a necessity that after every inactive period that you had to pull the heads, grind them, and reseat them and put it back together. They did this on at least two, if not three, of the main engines. We had four main engines and I think that they were working on three; that left

33

us with one for motion. That was our condition when they bombed Manila and it was a mad scramble to get those parts below deck because they were all laid out on canvas outside. It was so hot down below because we didn't have air conditioning. Well, we had some but it wasn't enough to cool. So they'd take the heads off the engines and carry them topside under an awning and work topside, you know, grind the valves and whatever they had to do with them. They took them inside to reassemble the engines and they were in time to get them down below.

The Japs bombed Pearl December 7th and December the 8th they bombed us. They did just as good a job of destroying facilities there as they did in Pearl. We didn't have an air force out there; the Japs destroyed that first day. Next day they destroyed the Navy Yard, destroyed their torpedo storage, they destroyed the dog-gone fuel oil storage. But just like at Pearl they didn't bomb submarines out there. They concentrated on the repair shops and the oil storage and that sort of thing. Turns out, big mistake.

Steve: Now were you in the middle of the bay when this was happening?

Ernie: Yeah, front row seat. Once the topside was clear we buttoned up and set her on the bottom. We played mud turtle in Manila Bay. The bay was not deep enough to completely hide the ship but it was deep enough where it had just the periscope sticking out of the water for air and that was it. Somehow the Japs missed that one in their bombing run. When they were bombing Cavite they were blowing massive explosions that the Skipper was watching through the periscope in the Control Room. He let some of us look through the scope at what was happening. I can remember him saying, "Good God Van!" Van Buskirk was our XO. He said, "Good God Van, look at this." Things were really blowing. They knew exactly where things were at, they knew exactly what they wanted to hit, and they proceed to do it.

Anyway, they just bombed us over but when the bombing rage was over we surfaced and commenced operations loading ship for war time load; for the torpedoes anyway.

The First War Patrol

Steve: How long did you stay in Manila after the Japanese attack?

Ernie: We got out of there on the 11th of December just after midnight and went on our first war patrol. We had to travel through the minefields at the entrance to Manila Bay at Corregidor and of course we had to go at night because of the Jap bombing and we went on three engines. One was still being put back together after overhaul. It took us until December 20th to get that No. 2 engine back together and run-in the bearings. The captain said in his War Patrol Report that "The best machinist's mates work at night and are making progress but it is slow work."¹ Then we lost the No. 3 engine on Christmas Eve; wiped crankshaft bearings and scored journals so back to three engines.

We got out of there and they sent us to up off of northern Luzon where they expected the Japanese to land, to patrol for, you know, and try to stop them.

Steve: Did you have the chance to attack any Japanese shipping?

Ernie: Yeah, but if it hadn't have been for bad torpedoes, why, things out there would have been very different. We fired on ships and they watched the blasted torpedoes go underneath the targets and not explode. Those magnetic exploders were supposed to explode when they went under the keel. And the darned things wouldn't do it. They'd pass under too deep and wouldn't explode and then you'd hear the explosion later after it had passed the ship. We attacked a steamer on the 25th and one torpedo hooked right and came back at the boat. That fish broached several times and exploded right near us caused us no damage; Merry Christmas!

Anyway, those bad fish really kept us from really decimating the Japanese transports when the war first started. They were allowed to land their blasted troops on all the islands out there and we couldn't do much about it. The submarines were the only line of defense.

Steve: Good point. I guess they underestimated them.

Ernie: We didn't have any luck there making contact so we shifted our patrol to off Formosa which is Taiwan now. Now that was better because we managed to sink one transport up there somewhere between Hong Kong and Formosa. After that they sent us back towards Manila Bay again; still nothing, and by this time we were running out of stores. We were running out of everything, especially fuel oil, because we hadn't really loaded up before the Japs bombed. Of course we couldn't go back to Manila so they ordered us to Darwin, Australia via Balikpapan to top off on fuel in Borneo. That oil that came out of the ground there was pure enough that you could burn it directly in diesel engines without purifying it. I mean, it was almost crystal clear.

Steve: No kidding?

Ernie: Absolutely beautiful oil. Maybe the Japs when they got it could burn it in their dog-gone Fire room boilers without doing anything to it. It's a really, really good grade of oil, natural oil. So anyway, we tanked up in Borneo before the Japs got there. And then we headed down through Makassar Strait and to Australia, Darwin, Australia. Which was in the northwest corner of

Australia. Desert town on the seacoast. By that time
the *Holland* and the *Otus*, submarine tenders, were
down there ahead of us so we went along side for a
refit. That ended our first war patrol. I think it was
two weeks maybe fifteen days refitting, for taking on
stores.

The Second War Patrol

Her first war patrol had lasted from December 11, 1941 to January 17, 1942. For the second war patrol the *Perch* was sent to the
area around the Celebes Island, specifically, Kendari Bay, to observe
and report on Japanese naval build-up in that area. After making
their report they were ordered to change their patrol station into the
Java Sea, north of Java. However tempting the targets were in
Kendari Bay, the shallow water inside this harbor would have necessitated a dangerous surface attack, so the *Perch* left this station and
headed for Java.

Steve: So it seems that you left on your second war patrol
around the beginning of February.

Ernie: That's right. First to Kendari Bay but we could do
nothing but look around. Too damn shallow for sub
ops. Then we headed towards Java.

Steve: So that was just a transit to the Java area?

Ernie: Anything but. During our transit we came upon what
looked like a lone Japanese merchant ship. Easy pickings. But as we made our approach on the surface she
let go at us, put a five-inch shell right through the fairwater, just forward of the Conning Tower. It went
right straight through it exploded in the doghouse but
didn't do a whole lot of damage, thank the Lord. But
it knocked out our radio transmitter because it ruptured the radio antennae trunk. And it knocked out
our hydraulic oil accumulator tank which at that
point in time was topside, just forward of the Conning

Tower. That was the real damage they did to us. Of course we made an emergency dive and got the heck out of there. We were able to fix the radio soon after.

Steve: Close call!

Ernie: Definitely was. We headed off after a report of Japanese troop transports heading to Java was received. After a run towards where they thought the landing would be we surfaced. It was nighttime on March 1st. We had been on the surface for about an hour or so when we spotted two Jap destroyers but far off, out of range, and heading away. We thought we were in the clear but they turned and headed back our way. During our set-up one of them damn destroyers turned straight at us. It was a full moon so maybe he saw our scope. Anyway we headed deep thinking we had about two-hundred feet beneath us but that water was shallow; we hit bottom at about 148 feet and so that destroyer started dropping depth charges as he passed over. The more they dropped depth charges the closer they came; the sucker dropped them right over us. The ship would jump up, and then settle back down after the explosion. It was a mess.

Caroline: Didn't you say that you didn't think you were going to die?

Ernie: No, I never thought that I was going to die. I guess I must have thought that I was protected, cause death never crossed my mind. The captain did some tricky maneuvering and we managed to sneak away from those two dogs. So we surfaced, started charging batteries and filling the air banks.

Steve: Any damage?

Ernie: We lost power to the port shaft and those depth charges hammered in the pressure hull in a number of different place. That was a bad beating they gave us. But there was worse to come.

Steve: Where did you go then? Did you continue on to look for the Japanese invasion transports?

38

Ernie:	Well, we did try. About two hours before sunrise on March 2nd we spotted two more Jap destroyers. Were they the same ones that caught us on the 1st? We never knew. The captain tried to hide by setting the boat on the bottom and turning off all our running machinery. Good idea; it didn't work. Those destroyers headed straight at us like we were marked on their charts. Once they got over us they commenced with depth charges.
Steve:	Was it just like continuous all day, or ...?
Ernie:	Well, it was not really continuous, because they have to make a new run. They pass over you and drop their depth charge and they continue onward and make a circular, a new run, pass over you again. They took turns doing that. It was pretty hairy. I never once thought that we were going to lose the ship.
Steve:	You did not?
Ernie:	No, I just didn't think that. I guess I was too young and ignorant.
Steve:	That's because you were a kid.
Ernie:	Yeah. Never thought we'd lose it. They went at us hard but steady maintaining sound contact all the while so there was no chance to slip away. One would make a run then the other would stand off. Brutal time. At that time the submarine sanitary tank had porcelain toilet bowls. Well the first close depth charge shattered those all to pieces. So now you're going to the bathroom in a four inch hole and no way to close it off. Not pleasant. Though those damn explosions released a lot of us of the need to make that trip to the head.
Steve:	How long did this go on?
Ernie:	They gave it to us all during the daylight hours that whole day. From the way they were dropping them, they seemed like to have dropped a buoy over where we were at; they pounded us right down into the mud. Later in the day I guess debris and oil may have come

to the surface so they thought they'd sunk us so they left. It took us more than an hour of blowing and working to break free of the bottom. We finally surfaced. The air was so dang bad you couldn't light a match. When we surfaced we only had one tank of air left; the others had ruptured during depth charging and either escaped outside or escaped inside the hull. Plenty came inside because we had a big pressure buildup in the hull. In fact, we had to hold onto the Quartermaster when he opened the hatch to keep him from getting pulled up through the hatch by all that air rushing up.

Steve: Unbelievable. Was that the only damage?

Ernie: I wish it had been. No, we were in terrible shape. We tried all four main engines and could only get one started. The reduction gears were pretty beat up. But that gave us about five knots headway. We also got the dinkie engine charging the batteries, such as they were. Lots of broken jars that had to be jumpered out. And there were grounds everywhere. We really took a terrible beating.

Steve: I am surprised you even made it to the surface.

Ernie: No more than we were. But the surface is no place for a sub so we prepared to try a running dive just before sunrise on March 3rd. And we were going down stern first, water was pouring in all the hatches: the Conning Tower hatch, the engine room hatch, and the three-inch circ water line was leaking where it went through the hull. You couldn't seat the hatches because they deformed from the depth charging. So we had to emergency surface from about seventy-five feet. That was a long, slow fight for the surface since we only had one tank of air left to blow. We tried resetting the dogs on the hatches but even with that you could still see through the closed hatch.

We had been on the surface only a short while when the OD reported that there were three Jap tin cans and two cruisers about three thousand, thirty-five hundred yards out ahead of us; they started to fire. The first salvo went over us, the second one fell short of us, and the Skipper alerted us that we probably would have to scuttle the boat if we couldn't dive and, at that point, we knew we couldn't. The torpedoes were no good; we had hot-runs in both rooms. The deck gun couldn't be trained; we were helpless on the surface. So he gave the word to abandon ship and scuttle ship, which we did.

Steve: Now, do you remember where you were when that order was given?

Ernie: Yeah, I do very well. I was down in the pump room, trying to reset the brushes on the AC motor generator because those old ropes were separating. You had the brushes that seated on the slip ring and those gave us our AC power. When the depth charge hits those brushes they would hop off and you've lost AC power completely. During a lull between Japanese depth charge attacks I was down there, directly below the control room, in the pump room. I was trying to reset the bushes on the motor generator when the OD passed the word, "Abandon ship!" There was no speaker down there, and I didn't hear it. Everyone was already off the ship, by the time I got the word that we were supposed to get off. And I almost got left behind.

Steve: How did you get the word?

Ernie: I don't know somebody hollered it out but I don't remember who it was.

Caroline: Probably it was Turk [Turner] who came for you.

Ernie: But I got off well, well, before the thing started to go down.

Steve: Now, that's got to be a terrible thing to hear. "Abandon ship." I mean ...

Ernie: It's about the worse feeling you could come up with I think, short of getting shot. That's your home and

41

you just don't think you're going to lose it till it's lost. It's a horrible thing to float off and away from the boat like that; she slowly settled and she just literally dove in the water beneath. It looked just like a regular dive except this time she did it without us.

Chapter 3 Notes:

1. D. A. Hurt., commanding, "USS Perch (SS 176), Report of First War Patrol". (Commander Submarine Force Pacific Fleet, 17 January 1942, typewritten and library bound, Book 176, Submarine Force Museum and Library, Groton, Connecticut), 2.

CHAPTER 4

THE LONG NIGHT BEGINS

The First of Twelve Hundred and Ninety Seven Days

THE *PERCH* HAD been overmatched by the array of Japanese naval forces and had been unable to dive. Even if the desire had been there, slugging it out with destroyers and cruisers on the surface was neither rational nor possible. As the official report described, "The submarine's [deck] gun was inoperative, and torpedoes could not be fired. Enemy depth charges had caused three of *Perch's* torpedoes to run in their tubes and the heat, exhaust gases and nervous tension resulting therefrom (*sic*) had aggravated the already extremely difficult conditions."[1]

Steve: Now, were you in just a life vest? Or were you in rubber boats, or just life vest?

Ernie: No, we were just floating with the life jackets. We were floating in water for about an hour. The destroyers came closer but they took their time. Maybe they thought it was a trap and we were the bait. We were pretty good bait too; a whole submarine crew to interrogate. The Japs on the destroyer *Ushio* picked us up one by one in their small boat; it was like a whale boat.

Caroline: Weren't you in the water long enough for somebody to ask what they eat?

Ernie: Yeah, yeah; we were in the water for about an hour. The sun was past noon when the last of us got picked up. That was my buddy Robison I think; it was somebody anyway. One person piped up and asked "When the Japs pick us up I wonder what they'll feed us?" And Robison answered "Rice you dummy; what else do Japs eat?" I replied "I hope it's with cream and sugar; cream and sugar because I can't eat plain rice!" Well, about two days later when we finally did get fed a meal it was plain rice; no cream, no sugar, but it was the best damn rice I ever had!"

Found by a member of the Submarine Force in the radio room of a Japanese Submarine. Translation of the Japanese on the back is, "Enemy personnel (adrift) picked up by our ship the day after Naval engagement off Surabaya."

Perch crew on the deck of the IJN *Ushio* after capture
http://www.navsource.org/archives/08/08176.htm

Here we are on the *Ushio*; a bunch of scared and confused kids. Right in the center of the photo is a guy who looks like he's having a smoke.

Steve: Yes. I see him.

Ernie: That's Robison. I am just to the left; all you can see is my hat and the top of my brow but that's me! We were on the *Ushio* all day, until nightfall, and then they transferred us; they were pretty good to us really. They gave us hardtack and some hot sake and water. At nightfall they transferred us to the *Op Ten Noort* which was a captured Dutch hospital ship that they'd made a prison ship out of; it looked like a hospital ship with the red crosses and all but there was nothing medical going on. They had maybe one thousand crew members from British ships that had sunk off Singapore and had the crews of a couple of Dutch cruisers, English cruisers that they had sunk; one was the HMS *Exeter*.

OP TEN NOORT prewar, later HIKAWA MARU NO. 2
"StateLibQld 1 145623 Op Ten Noort (ship)"
Item is held by John Oxley Library, State Library of Queensland.
Licensed under Public Domain.

They put us down in the coal hold. There was only one exit out with an armed guard at the exit. There was no water down there no facilities no nothing. After, I think it was two days or three days they finally got around to giving us some food. It was rice and prunes cooked together and it was darned good I tell you; hunger improves the flavor! God, it was better than any apple pie but that was the only meal we got. Water was the real problem because the source of water was topside and the Japs wouldn't let you go up to get it. Finally they started letting one man at a time go to get water. Christ, we probably had over a thousand prisoners down in the hold. Some of those men were badly burned and didn't get water for three or four days. They had no clothing to speak of and those with third degree burns, their skin was just blisters; it was a horrible mess. I don't remember how long we were on the *Op Ten Noort*, at least three or four days anyway. It was hard to tell one day from the next.

Capture and Incarceration

The prisoners were offloaded and marched, many barefoot, through the streets of Makassar. This city is almost on the equator so the blacktop streets were hot enough to cause the feet of the column of marching men to burn, blister, and bleed. Before heading for their final destination, the officers and certain key enlisted men, like the Radiomen, were removed and ultimately spent their imprisonment in camps on the home islands of Japan. The remaining enlisted men marched to a former Dutch army training camp that the Japanese had made into a detention facility for Allied prisoners. The *Perch* men were not the only Americans to be interned here. Survivors of the USS *Pope* (DD 225), a World War I era four-stack destroyer that had been sunk on March 1 as part of the same battle that claimed the *Perch*, later called the Battle of the Java Sea, were also brought to the camp.

Ernie: After about four days we pulled into Makassar, Celebes. They off-loaded all of the Allied prisoners and marched us through the city. It was daytime and Makassar is about a half a degree off the equator. It was as hot as hell as we waited to get off the *Op Ten Noort* but that was the good part. Once we were off the ship they marched all of us through the city to what would be our first prison camp. Those blacktop streets were already hot; so you could have fried an egg on them. Most of us didn't have shoes so they marched barefoot across that frying pan.

Caroline: Didn't you say before that getting there the pavement was so hot that ones who didn't have shoes had blisters on the bottom of their feet?

Ernie: I was fortunate enough to have shoes but the guys who didn't? You could hardly look at their feet they were so awful; all blistered and bleeding. Terrible.

Caroline: Didn't one of the officers have a funny shoe story?

Ernie: Yeah, Jake Vandergrift; he had what looked to be the oldest pair of shoes. They were falling apart. His old steamers. And somebody said to him "Mr. Vandergrift, why didn't you wear good shoes when we abandoned ship?" "Oh" He said, "I didn't want to get them wet."

Steve: What a character. Kept his good humor I guess. Well, so they marched you through the streets to the prison camp.

Ernie: That's right. They marched us through the city to what was a former Dutch training camp, troop camp, army camp which they'd made into a prison camp. There was a guard at every street junction on the way to … we didn't know to where.

Steve: Now, did you see any of the local people when you were heading to the camp?

Ernie: Along the road. They said the Japs were so rough on everybody that they had to show enthusiasm to stay out of trouble. So they showed up and as long as they cheered, the Japs were okay with 'em. So they cheered and watched us monkeys walking through town. They cheered the Japs but they didn't seem that happy about it.

We finally arrived at the camp. Honestly, the camp facilities weren't that bad as they were. It was an old Dutch military training camp so it was well built and had all the things you might need. There were good water facilities because you had city water and good head facilities but that was about it. You took a bath in a crude fashion, and the toilet facilities were crude, but far different than what we would become accustomed to later. The head was, well, instead of a toilet like we have they had a slit trench, two bricks cemented to the edges on each side. You squatted on the brick, that's where you went to the bathroom.

	This is a drawing of just that made by a Machinist's Mate Third Class off the *Pope* named Philip Raymond "Shorty" Nagele. He was from Louisiana and was something of an artist.
Steve:	How was he able to draw, and more so, keep these pictures in the camp?
Ernie:	He didn't. He made very tiny drawings that he could hide, I understand. Then when we were freed he had the time to draw them correct size and he used the little sketches to remind him. He was really quite good. So anyway, we were there for, well I was there until they moved us into another camp in, I think early '44.
Steve:	Did they just leave you in the camp for awhile, or did they put you right to work?
Ernie:	No. They just left us in the camp, really, for a spell. I don't remember how many days it was.
Steve:	Sure.
Ernie:	That we were … They didn't bother us at all, just left us in the camp. In the very beginning the prisoners, both English and Australian and some Dutch, organized a band because there had been all kinds of musical instruments left behind, probably by the Dutch. So, there were some of them that could play those things so they organized a band. They were having a hell of a good time playing music 'till the doggone Japs heard the music and came charging. So they beat their butts for playing music and they confiscated the instruments. That was the way you found out you couldn't do things; they beat you.
Caroline:	I'm curious, because you didn't start working parties for several months. So, what did you do initially?
Ernie:	I don't think it was several months; it was more like weeks, and they just gradually built up their nerve, I think, to take prisoners on working parties. Also, I don't think the Japanese expected prisoners. It was not something that they had anticipated. Caught

49

	them by surprise you would say. So the city jail was full and old warehouses, garages, it was curious.
Steve:	So when you got there, to Makassar, there were other prisoners of war already there.
Ernie:	Yeah. There were some Dutch prisoners and some English and Australian. The process of consolidating all the prisoners in one place had begun but was no way completed when we arrived.
Steve:	When did the men from the *Pope* get there?
Ernie:	They were there not long after us *Perch* guys arrived. They were in much worse shape than we were, because they'd been in the water for more than a day; covered with oil and such. It started out there pretty hot for them. That was the old *Pope*. Poor suckers.
Steve:	Before we get into any specifics, I wanted to ask you, what was a typical day like? Nothing special, just like a regular day.
Ernie:	In prison camp?
Steve:	Yes.
Ernie:	Up, I guess about 6:30 am. Got dressed. Ate at 7:00. Most of us went on working parties to different parts of the town.
Steve:	What did you eat? Just rice?
Ernie:	The food was, not much of it. The first months we were probably on Dutch stores that were captured. Bakery was a hamburger bun. A hamburger bun, that's what you got. And then they started giving us watery rice for breakfast and then in the evening, a small cup of rice. That went on for, I don't know, three or four months and we finally convinced them that we had to have three meals a day because that was what we were used to. So they started giving us another cup of rice at noon. It was just about a coffee cup of rice is what it was.
Steve:	What was that for breakfast? Watery rice?
Ernie:	Breakfast was a brew of rice. They cooked rice until it dissolved into starch.

Steve:	Okay.
Ernie:	Part grain and part starch.
Steve:	Right.
Ernie:	They called it *bubur*.
Steve:	They called it what?
Ernie:	*Bubur*. That's what the locals called it.
Steve:	*Bubur*. Is that a Japanese word maybe?
Ernie:	I think it's Javanese. There wasn't much taste to it.
Steve:	No.
Ernie:	That's where we used to steal cane for sugar. What else? Basically it was a very skimpy simple diet. It was soft rice at breakfast, the *bubur*. Occasionally a piece of what we called stink fish. I don't know what that fish was, but we called it stink fish because it did stink.
Steve:	Stink fish?
Ernie:	It was dried fish. Sun dried and then they just boiled it. You get that; you'd have to flip the maggots out of it where flies had landed.
Steve:	Right. What about other meals?
Ernie:	There was the stink fish which was most often at breakfast but sometimes at other meals. Then the other times, there was rice, some kind of vegetable, and occasionally, I guess, a piece of meat. Not often. Not every day. At night, it was the same thing again.
Steve:	When we had talked before, you said the first things they fed you were what you thought were old Dutch provisions, Dutch food?
Ernie:	Yeah, I think it must have been, because there were boll weevils, rice worms. The Japs made no effort to separate the worms from the rice, so, when you got your ration, it was composed of rice worms and rice. Yeah. You take them out, and when you take them out, you still discovered that you had as many worms as you had rice. After a few meals of going hungry, you began to eat. You no longer sorted, you just ate whatever was in

that bowl. That's what we ate; rice and worms steamed together. After a while you think that it tastes good. Worms didn't bother us a bit.

Caroline: You said you figured it was good protein, right?

Ernie: Yeah, it just quickly became a normal thing. Sometimes we could get, buy a stalk of bananas from a native. But the Japs never fed us bananas, but sometimes they'd let Indonesian merchants come to the gate ... and, you know, sell whatever they were peddling, usually it was peanut brittle candy and bananas. Mostly that's what it was that the Japs would allow.

Caroline: But that wasn't right away.

Ernie: What?

Caroline: That wasn't right away, was it?

Ernie: No, it wasn't. The first 30 days, why, we were just sorta there and nobody was allowed to come close. Oh, and we used to get a cup of coffee, black coffee, for each meal.

Steve: Could you tell if it was real coffee?

Ernie: I think it was real coffee, yeah, because they grew it on the island.

Steve: Oh yeah.

Ernie: I think it was. It wasn't bad coffee.

Steve: Not bad?

Ernie: No, it wasn't.

Steve: You said you got up in the morning and you got dressed.

Ernie: Got up in the morning, yeah. Somebody hollered reveille at about 6:30 am. If I remember right, the Jap guard used to come in the barracks and holler reveille. Then somebody then in the barracks would take over to make sure everybody was up.

Steve: Okay. What did you wear? Did you continue to wear your *Perch* clothes? They couldn't have lasted the whole time.

Ernie: No. Those were taken away. Working clothes were given to us. It was unbleached muslin. Shorts, with

52

drawstring belt, for belt. They were basically shaped like our underwear is shaped without the short sleeve, and that was it. No underclothing. Which was fine because it was just that hot.

Steve: Oh. Now did they give you those made, or did you have to make them?

Ernie: They gave them to us, ready-made.

Steve: Okay. What about shoes?

Ernie: Shoes were non-existent. They gave us what we called clip-clops, clogs, which were wooden. Wooden shoes just with a strap across the toes.

Steve: I see.

Ernie: That's what they gave us.

Steve: Now what about, not that you came with any, but what about personal belongings? Were you able to keep personal belongings?

Ernie: What you had on your back. The Dutch men came with a full seabag. But we weren't that fortunate. We had what we had on our back. So most of the guys were barefoot.

Steve: Who came with a full seabag? Who was it that came with a full sea bag?

Ernie: The Dutch.

Steve: Dutch?

Ernie: Yeah. Well, they were, they were posted on the island, so most of them even went to the bank before the Japs took over and took the money and divided it amongst themselves and then hid it. So they had money all during the war.

Caroline: Pretty smart.

Ernie: And it's what we needed to get from them. They had the money, we needed the money. So we used to buy stuff from the natives, smuggle it in through the gate to the camp and then sell it to the Dutchmen for exorbitant prices. They wouldn't smuggle anything through the gate, wouldn't take a chance on getting caught. We were bolder and, truthfully, we had no other choice. So we ended up with their money. But, of course that was a bit later on too. We all were pretty green at first. Just sort of sat around the prison barracks for the first month. Figuring things out, thinking about how it all could have gone different. It couldn't have, of course. But that doesn't stop you thinking about it.

Chapter 4 Notes:

1. *United States Submarine Losses – World War II*. Washington: U. S. Government Printing Office, 1946. Revised and reissued as NAVPERS 15,784 in 1949, 26.

CHAPTER 5

THE DRY SEASON: APRIL TO OCTOBER, 1942

Establishing the Routine and Forced Labor

THE GEOGRAPHY, PROXIMITY to the equator, and abundance of warm seawater cause the climate of the island of Celebes to be unvarying tropical. The days vary in length by less than an hour over the course of the year. Temperatures average around 82 degrees Fahrenheit and are uniformly coupled with high humidity. All of these factors cause the climate to be mostly unchanging over the course of the year. The only factor that determines a change in season is the rain.

The Dry Season lasts from April to October and the Wet Season from November to March although, as with all weather patterns, annual variations invariably occur. In the prison camp days, months, and years became somewhat meaningless as the duration of the incarceration, toil, and torture dragged on endlessly. The only varying aspect of this quasi-life was whether it was wet or whether it was dry.

Steve: So when did you start the forced labor? When was the first working party?

Ernie: I think it must have been a good month after we were settled in camp before they started taking us out on working parties. In the beginning, it was only a few people that went. As the Japs consolidated what they'd captured, and we felt more resigned with where we were, they began to organize more working parties. Part of the way it worked is a Jap petty officer or a non-commissioned office at the facility would request a working party from Jap headquarters. If it was approved they would send a guard, or sometimes two guards, to the camp entrance and count off the number of workers that they wanted for that day. Then they'd march you to the work site. We of course had no idea where we were going in those first few days. We didn't know if we were in a good working party, or a poor working party, or what it would be. Some turned out be humane and some turned out to be pretty cruel. It just all depended.

Steve: If you remember, what was the first working party that you went on?

Ernie: I think the first one I was on was offloading and loading ships, the Japanese supply ships that were coming in. Here is a drawing by Shorty showing how we did it. We are coaling that ship and all by manual labor.

There were a lot of ships at first, it seemed, since that island had just recently been occupied. I guess they needed all the things to set up their organization. The number of ships died down after a while but in the beginning they used almost all of us to unload their damn ships.

Steve: How about after that? What kind of work did they have you doing next?

Ernie: Well then we started tearing down walls of bombed out buildings and salvaging the brick. And we did that a lot. There were plenty of bombed out buildings, again from the Jap invasion.

So they had knocked them down and then had us clean them up. They were big on cleaning. And of course reusing the brick, which we did later.

Steve: That sounds like terrible work to be doing in that heat.

Ernie: Terrible is the word. Heavy, dirty, dry and dangerous. The buildings were unstable and the dust from the bricks we chipped off was awful. You breathed it in, what choice did you have? And as hot as you can imagine. Guys fell down all the time. We got a bit

used to it over time but at first we dropped like flies. Oh they got us back up quick enough.

Steve: Were all the working parties as bad?

Ernie: Most. But occasionally you would get a good one. Like we'd have a working party sent to the city park cutting grass. They had us use a strip of bamboo as a cutter. It's sharp, it's pretty good as a cutter; it splits, it's tough, so that's what we used as grass cutters. And we'd lie there on this great big field and we'd creep along, cutting grass. Lying down at work was nice, the grass was nice. Still hot as hell but something different and nowhere near as bad as hauling bricks in the dust.

Steve: Did they make the officers work as well?

Ernie: They took our officers off to Japan in September of '42. They left one officer behind to act as our POW commander. Just one. He was off of the *Pope* and was not required to do manual work.

Steve: So the Perch officers were sent to Japan?

Ernie: Yes; that was my belief. That was not a pleasure cruise. The Japs assumed that officers and Radiomen had secret information so, when they could find them, they would send them to Japan for special interrogation. Can you imagine that? Awful.

Steve: I can't imagine what that was like. Separation from the crew must have been awful as well. Now you said that they would take Radiomen "when they could find them." What did you mean by them.

Ernie: Officers were easy to identify; different uniforms. Radiomen? Who knows? They knew the Japs had it in for the Radiomen so most of the Radiomen kept quiet and didn't confess their rate. They just said they were something else.

Steve: I understand. Were there any other unusual work parties during that first Dry Season? I can imagine that there might be some tasks you could do when it was dry that could not be done when it was wet.

Ernie:	Steve, you are exactly right. I believed I mentioned the last time or the time before about the Dutch concrete pill boxes that you moved.
Steve:	Yes. Were you involved in that?
Ernie:	Yeah, whenever there were areas that needed defending along the beach the Dutch had built these pillboxes for machine guns and the like. Well, the Japs didn't like where they were so we had to move them inland a ways.
Steve:	Were these like the classic concrete round pillboxes that you might see in the movies?
Ernie:	Exactly like that.
Steve:	It doesn't seem possible that something that heavy could be moved.
Ernie:	They could and they were. If you put enough slaves on it I think you can move anything. Anyway, we moved those monsters.
Steve:	What was the process? Surely not just pull and pull?
Ernie:	Lots of that of course. But we got coconut palm tree log rollers underneath them and then tied ropes around the thing and we dragged it, I don't know how far. Along the beach and even further inland to relocate them away from being right on the beach. Some Japanese genius strategy I'm sure. Here is another of Shorty's artwork that shows it pretty well. God, they were hell to get started moving.

Steve: Yes, that shows just what you described. But is that a Japanese soldier on top of it?

Ernie: Yup. Directing traffic; along for the ride. That was about typical. He's not worried about the extra weight.

Escape Attempt

Steve: With that kind of treatment and the hard labor you described didn't anyone try to escape?

Ernie: Three Dutch guys did attempt to escape. They made arrangements with the native chief because they were Dutch men and they'd been station there before the war. They thought they knew who they were dealing with. The chief was asked to provide a boat and a crew to sail and such and take the prisoners to Australia and he readily agreed to that for a certain amount of money. What our camp commander said was that the chief went immediately to the Japanese and told them what he had been asked to do and where the boat was going to be waiting. When the prisoners left the camp and got on the boat, or started to board the boat, damn Jap guards stepped right out and took control. They brought them back to jail and beat the hell out of them. This drawing shows that event. Those guards were pretty ingenious with their beatings.

Then, they put them in the brig for a couple or three days; I don't really remember how long. Every day they would take them out and beat them again. When they changed watch, they beat them. Their watch was three hours instead of four hours. Then, at the end of the three days, they took them off somewhere. The natives told us that they took them out to be killed and to bury them. We had only the natives' word for what they've done with them.

Caroline: Didn't they have to dig their own graves?

Ernie: Yeah. They made them dig their own grave and when
               they were done they blindfolded them and then made
               them kneel down and chopped their heads off. After
               this was done the Japs made us assemble. They told
               us for any more escape attempts those who try would
               be beaten, tortured and killed and the closest neigh-
               bors in the camp would get the same treatment. This
               potentially made a rat out of everyone so that pretty
               much stopped the escapes. Everyone was watching
               everyone.

CHAPTER 6

THE WET SEASON:
NOVEMBER 1942 TO MARCH 1943

Adjusting to Life as a Prisoner

ERNIE AND THE other prisoners attempted to use their own ingenuity to supplement their diet, when occasion and opportunity allowed. Sometimes this would be through the acquisition of extra foodstuffs of the type they were already eating. On other occasions more exotic items found their way onto the prison menu.

Steve: Did you manage to augment your diet with any extra things?

Ernie: Yeah: with the commodore's cat.

Steve: What was that?

Ernie: We caught and ate the commodore's cat.

Steve: Tell me more about that.

Ernie: Well, that was early '43, yeah. Now you would think that the Commodore and his cat were at some distance from the prisoners and they both were, but that damn cat didn't have sense enough to stay outside the camp. He was a rover; he roamed all over. One day he roamed in the wrong place. Now he did come into our barracks a couple of times, and our guys said "Next time he comes in...we'll get him!"

Steve: And then?

Ernie: He came back, they captured him and skinned him. Just that quick.

Caroline:	Oh, gross. Did you kill him first? Ernie? You captured him; you must've killed him before you skinned him.
Ernie:	Well, yeah. That goes along with skinning. He got killed almost as soon as he got captured. They were trying to make a hat out of him. We ended up feeding the cat to the prisoners. The Commodore never did find out where his cat went. He'd probably would have chopped some heads off if he knew where his cat went.
Caroline:	Didn't you cook him?
Ernie:	We caught him, we killed him, we skinned him, we ate him.
Steve:	Was it roasted? Boiled? Grilled? Did you grill it? How did you cook it?
Ernie:	If I remember right, we turned him over to the galley and they cooked him with the cooking rice. By this time the prisoners were running the galley. One of our guys, Van Horn, an electrician, was running the galley and... I don't remember who else was there. The galley guys were kind of people you never saw. You know, you went to work, you slept, you went to work. They were working in the food line all the time.
Caroline:	What did the cat taste like? Do you remember?
Ernie:	Just like good meat. You know, we got away with it and there was no retaliation. This was pretty early on. If it had been later it may have been worse for us. They might not have been able to find us specifically, so maybe they would have punished the whole camp. That would have been awful. Later on that cat might have killed some of us.
Caroline:	Our cat just left the room after hearing that story!
Ernie:	That's the only cat I ever ate!
Steve:	Any other unusual items in your diet?
Ernie:	You'd have to say that the eggshell weren't quite normal.
Steve:	Eggshells?

Ernie:	Yup. Every once in a while we'd get some eggs; some came from the guards and some from trading. We would cook with the egg, of course, but then the cooks would keep the shells, grind them up, and mix them into our rice mash.
Steve:	Why would they do that? Not for nutrition.
Ernie:	I don't know who came up with the idea but they thought that they would use eggshells ground up to eat as a calcium supplement. Almost never saw anything dairy. I can't prove it but I believe that was responsible for the Perch men preserving their teeth, their bones, and their posture later on due to that extra calcium. None of us lost any teeth; not from just falling out anyway.
Steve:	That's amazing. I guess that could work.
Ernie:	Seems like it did. I still had most of my choppers when the war was over.
Steve:	Excellent! Now I believe you had said once that during this time they took a group of men to Kendari to work in a mine. Is that right?
Ernie:	Yes. They took a draft to eastern Celebes, Kendari, where they were working a lead mine, I guess, or copper mine. They took, I think it was two hundred that went to work in that damn mine. They were there a little less than a year and less than a hundred came back; they lost over fifty percent to starvation and disease. Worked 'em to death.
Steve:	Of course you weren't selected?
Ernie:	No thank God. No *Perch* men went on that draft.
Steve:	That's fortunate. It sounds like they were awfully treated.
Ernie:	Yes, there was plenty of that, but every once in a while the Japs would do something that would make you scratch your head.
Steve:	How do you mean?

Ernie:	Well, they organized working parties early on to clean up the damaged areas of the city. They asked for volunteers, and I didn't volunteer, but some of our people did. This one job was reclaiming brick from burned out skeletons of a badly bomb-damaged building, and that was when one of the *Pope* crewmen was killed when a wall fell on him. Well we expected they would just cart him off but all the work was stopped. They organized and treated him with a regular military funeral with an American flag. He even laid in state and the damn Jap admiral came and paid his respects; bowed and treated him just like he was one of their own people because he had died working for the Emperor. Then they buried him someplace.
Caroline:	That was because he died working for the Empire.
Ernie:	Right. Died working for the Japanese, yeah; an honorable death. He was the only person that they honored with a military funeral.
Steve:	First the rough day to day treatment, then, that kind of ceremony. It must have been hard to put those two things together.
Ernie:	Yeah, that was the only case of that that I knew of where they did that. Usually they just beat the hell out of you.

Bonding as a Crew

Steve:	You said all the *Perch* men were together but did you have a smaller crew of your own that you stayed with?
Ernie:	Yes. A bunch of us hung together. First of course was "Turk" Turner; Marion Turner. He was probably my best friend, before and after. Then there was Jesse Robison, called Robbie, Dan Crist and Ancil Winger. Gordon Clevinger was with us at first. We called Gordon "Sleepy" but he left the group to work in our galley.

Steve:	Clevinger is listed as a coxswain. What was a coxswain's job on the boats?
Ernie:	All I remember is he was a torpedo instructor.
Steve:	Why was he called Sleepy?
Ernie:	Because of his eyes. He looked Sleepy. That was his nickname: Sleepy. His eyes, eyelids drooped. He looked like he was half asleep when he wasn't. He got lots of pokes from the Japs because they always thought he was sleeping on the job.
Steve:	Anyone else we're missing?
Ernie:	Well, did I say Harper? Earl Harper?
Steve:	No.
Ernie:	Can't forget Harper. That's the crew then: Turk Turner, Robbie Robison, Dan Crist, Ancil Winger, and Earl Harper. Oh yeah, and Ernie "The Kid" Plantz; that's us boys.
Steve:	So it was just *Perch* men in your group?
Ernie:	Yes. Except for Brown; Fred Brown from off the old *Asheville*. He was the only survivor off of that ship so we sort of adopted him.
Caroline:	The only survivor?
Ernie:	Yup. The *Asheville* was an old Asiatic Fleet gunboat.[1] She got jumped the day after the Perch went down and two Jap destroyers blasted the hell out of her. Not much of a match. Brown said that there were lots of survivors in the water but the Japs only picked him up. No sense to that. He ended up on the *Op Ten Noort* with us and, being alone, just sort of got adopted.
Steve:	Did he stay with you the whole time in camp?
Ernie:	Up until his end. He died in March of 1945 during the bad times; the last of a crew of over one hundred and sixty men. Probably were a bunch of refugees too that never got counted.
Steve:	What a story.
Ernie:	Brown was a good shipmate.

Steve:	Did you guys have jobs to do around the barracks when you weren't on a working party?
Ernie:	Yes, that's right. We divided up the household chores! Turner and I were the brave ones maybe because we were the youngest. Me and Turk were always looking to smuggle something in all the time. We took a chance.
Caroline:	I remember. Turk and you were the best ones at that.
Ernie:	Robbie kept the place clean.
Caroline:	Sleepy, what did he do? What did Sleepy do in the group?
Ernie:	Remember? He abandoned ship and went to cook at the galley. I couldn't have blamed him really. If I had been offered the chance to do it, I'd have done it, I'm sure, you know, it'd be close to the food.
Steve:	How about Crist?
Ernie:	Yeah.
Steve:	Crist? What'd he do?
Ernie:	I really can't remember. He moved out of our group but I don't know why.
Steve:	Winger?
Ernie:	Winger was the washer. If our clothes needed washing, he washed clothes. Robbie was the house cleaner mostly. They seemed to help each other out. Which was a full-time job, really.
Steve:	We got a job for everyone except Crist.
Ernie:	I do not remember what Crist did. I cannot remember for the life of me. But everybody worked for the group; nobody was sacking out when things needed to be done.
Steve:	Did you have a name? Did you have a name for the group? Something like the Dirty Dozen?
Ernie:	No.
Steve:	No? No, just a group?
Ernie:	No special name. We weren't that well organized!

Chapter 6 Notes:

1. USS *Asheville* (PG-21) was a gunboat of 1,700 tons (loaded) that was commissioned in 1920. She saw service as a part of the Asiatic Fleet with extensive service in China as a member of the Yangtze Patrol and in the Philippines. She was sunk in the aftermath of the Battle of the Java Sea on March 3, 1942. [http://www.navsource.org/archives/12/09021.htm]

CHAPTER 7

THE DRY SEASON:
APRIL TO OCTOBER, 1943

ERNIE HAD SURVIVED the first year of captivity at the hands of the Japanese military. Though conditions were harsh and supplies were frugal they had established a cohesive band of shipmates and were acclimating to a life in prison. The old Dutch camp with its relatively modern construction and sanitation facilities helped maintain a semblance of good health. Though hard work in the burning sun, periodic beatings, and short rations were the order of the day, the men of the *Perch* were holding their own.

During this season the Japanese continue to hold sway over the majority of Greater East Asia Co-Prosperity Sphere, their plan to create a self-sufficient "bloc of Asian nations led by the Japanese and free of Western powers."[1] but the Allies are beginning to chip away at the Empire. In the first two months of the year, just prior to the beginning of the Dry Season, the Allies took back New Guinea and the Japanese were completely driven off of Guadalcanal. On April 18th Japanese Admiral Isoroku Yamamoto, architect of the attack on Pearl Harbor, is shot down and killed on his way to Bougainville.

Prisoners moved to a New Camp

Steve: What happened after the Wet Season ended?

Ernie: That's when we started construction on the new camp. The Japs got themselves pretty well organized and they were starting to train a self-defense group to take over the police duties; they called it "The Indonesian Force." And then they started to drill and train those

69

people and they decided that the camp we were living in was a military camp, and it was made with tiled decks, and tiled roofs, good ventilation, you know; it was a decent place. That's where they wanted to quarter those inductees, or whatever you want, the self-defense people. So, if they were going there, why we had to go. So that's when they started us building our own camp, so the defense force could move in. It was quite a project, clearing the land and building that thing, I'll tell you, because of those coconut trees growing all over the place at random, and all kinds of thick brush. We had to clear the whole damn thing and so build our own camp. Our new camp was not built out of brick and tile it was built out of bamboo and Nipa. Nipa was plaited, you know, into a mat.

Steve: Nipa? What is Nipa?

Ernie: It is sort of a scrub palm. We could split the fronds and weave them into a sort of panel, into a woven mat. So they had us clear the land and build a bamboo camp, about a mile south from where we were originally at. Unfortunately they chose an area that was wet in the rainy season. The Dutch had always quarantined it because of the presence of malaria and dysentery but that's where they had us build our camp. You could mark the decline of our health from the day we moved there. Two rainy seasons in that damn, soggy camp. The winter, the rainy season, of '44, '45, that's when most of our people died.

Steve: Do you think they deliberately chose that spot?

Ernie: No, I don't think so. I don't think it made any difference to them. I don't really think they thought about it too much at all because, after all, the guards had to live in the same area to watch us.

Steve: Oh, okay, right.

Ernie: This is a beautiful map of the camp that Dr. Borstlap made. He was quite an artist.

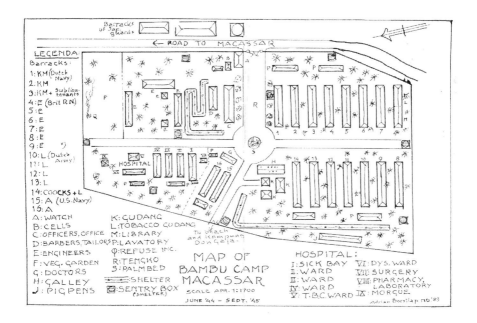

Steve: I'll say! That's very detailed.

Ernie: Anyway it was pretty rough because we built it during the Dry Season but during the rainy season the water would stand in some of the barracks a foot deep. You slept on boards that were up on a rack. That was a beautiful breeding place for mosquitoes.

Steve: Right. Of course; standing water.

Ernie: What was worse was that the septic tank and the well were too close together and when the water rose it contaminated the well water. So guys would get malaria and then get dysentery and we always were on the edge of starvation so we were weak and they'd die of either dysentery or malaria. It didn't much matter which. The Wet was the worst.

Steve: I can't imagine. Now during this Dry Season were there any memorable events?

Ernie: Well during this time the Japs decided to build a railroad from Makassar to Kendari. Now Kendari was where their airport was on the westerly side of the island. I don't know, I guess it was about thirty-five or forty kilometers between them with coconut groves and hills and sand dunes and whatever; very varied terrain. The prisoners had to dig out and lay the railbed all along the way. It was a pretty gruesome, gruesome task, trying to put down a foundation for a railroad in that heat and that terrain.

Steve: Now, were you involved in this?

Ernie: No, I was not, thank God. Awful lot of guys involved in that didn't come back.

Steve: We've talked about a couple of awful things. Did any less terrible things happen during this time?

Ernie: Well, there was the fishing party.

Caroline: Oh yes, Ernie! Tell him about that.

Ernie: Well we were always complaining about wanting more food to the guards.

Steve: Wasn't that dangerous?

Ernie: It was but we got where we could sort of read them. You knew which ones you could push a little and which ones to avoid. Sometimes we guessed wrong but mostly we kept on the pressure. We were always hungry.

Working with the Camp Guards

Ernie: So there was this *Kempeitai*...
Steve: I'm sorry, what was that? *Kempeitai*?
Ernie: Yes. A military policeman but more like a Nazi Gestapo. Mean and tricky.
Steve: Okay.
Ernie: Right, so he says, "You guys like to fish?" We answered "Sure, who doesn't, we're American." He says, "I'll see if I can take you on a fishing party some Sunday." "Oh, okay." So we forgot all about it. I don't know if it was that next Sunday or when, later a Jap guard comes to the American barracks. He wanted to know if the Americans wanted to go fishing. Sure, everybody volunteered to go fishing. So he marched us down to the gate and here comes a bunch of dang Jap recruit guards carrying shovels and burlap bags and wicker baskets. They marched us to where there was an abandoned fish hatchery, fish ponds, probably half acre ponds. The Japs decided they were going to have the prisoners build an earthen dam across the center of one of these ponds, and then bail the water from one side to the other so they could get the fish. So we went to work bailing the water and building the dam and weren't working fast enough for the Japs. They'd come along and whack you on the back with a piece of bamboo, to work harder. And this doggone *Kempeitai* spoke English; he's standing there on the bank watching. He says, "You wanted to go fishing?" he

says, "Now fish you bunch of bastards!" So that was our big party. You can imagine what that water was like: hot, stinking, sticky and crawling with things you don't want to know! Well once we got them fish corralled they called in some Englishmen and Dutchmen to help bail and between the three nationalities we got the thing bailed out until it was just stinking mud and fish flopping. So they gathered up the big fish and the Japs took them for their table and they gave us the little ones. We took them to the galley. The only way we had of cooking ours was to boil them but they smelled so bad of that stinky mud that we couldn't eat them. Not even us hungry, starving prisoners could eat them. The cooks just threw them out. However, the Japs filleted, breaded and fried their big fish and they all ended up with the squirts. So we got the last laugh on them. That ended up to be a good fishing party because we got a good laugh watching them suffer because those stinky fish made them so sick!

Caroline:	Serves them right! You were the smart ones.
Ernie:	Amen. Well, but really we couldn't even try to eat them hungry as we were. It was just too awful. Maybe there were some worms or maggots in those fish from being trapped in that fishpond. Good thing we didn't have nice breading to disguise that nasty flavor and smell. Those fish might have killed some of us weaker ones.
Steve:	That *Kempeitai* sounds like an evil character.
Ernie:	Without a doubt. We managed to tweak his nose a time or two.
Steve:	How so?
Ernie:	This *Kempeitai* used to come around when we were on working party and, he spoke excellent English, and he would talk to some of the guys. He'd seem very friendly and he'd try to get them to give him information. To my knowledge no one ever did. He singled out a Filipino steward that we had. His nickname was

"Ping". Macario Sarmiento was his whole name but we called him Ping.

Steve: How did he get that nickname?

Ernie: I don't know. Anyway he, the *Kempeitai* said, "You don't like the Americans, do you?" I guess because Ping's skin was a little darker he thought he wasn't American. The Japs forced a lot of people who weren't Japanese to work for them and he figured that was the situation here I guess. So Ping played along and said, "Well, I don't know." He said, "I haven't made up my mind. I've only been in the Navy twenty-seven years!"

Steve: Twenty-seven years?

Ernie: Right. You get it, and we got it, but the *Kempeitai* wasn't getting the joke. So he said "Well, you know if you help me," he says, "I'm in a position to help you." He says, "You have a family in Manila, do you?" "Oh yes" Ping said. The *Kempeitai* says, "Well, if anything happened to you, why, who'd take care of them?" "Oh," Ping said, "if anything happened to me she'd be a rich widow. I've got insurance with Uncle Sam, $10,000!" The *Kempeitai* finally caught on and stormed away mad. That was old Ping. He was a great guy.

Steve: Wonderful! Ping must have been one of the older of your shipmates.

Ernie: I think he was the oldest one in the crew. He was in his fifties. Bald head as you could get. One time, before the war we were operating, the dry store room and the dang refrigerator and cold spot were adjacent to each other. And he went down the cold room, no, the dry stores to get some sugar, and the cold room hatch was closed when he went down. While he was down there somebody opened the hatch to the dang refrigerator. He stepped out of one hole and right down into the cold room refrigerator and this bowl of sugar he was carrying ended up right on top of his

head. Never seen a Filipino cuss like that I tell you!
Oh, Lordy!

Chapter 7 Notes:

1. William Theodore De Bary, *Sources of East Asian Tradition: The modern period* (New York: Columbia University Press, 2008), 622.

CHAPTER 8

THE WET SEASON: NOVEMBER 1943 TO MARCH 1944

THE JAPANESE GUARDS, considering the prisoners as something less than human, relied on violence, cruelty, and a baseball bat to communicate their intentions. Absent a common language, prisoners discovered where the "boundaries" were by the beatings that occurred once the boundaries were crossed. Incidents that occasioned the use of the bat for a beating allowed the prisoners to develop a mental rule book about what was allowed and what was forbidden. Plantz believed that the Japanese authorities treated the prisoners so inhumanely because they had disgraced themselves by choosing to be captured instead of dying in battle or by their own hand. This voluntary loss of honor had set the Americans apart from their family and nation, in the eyes of the guards, and rendered them unworthy of normal human care and consideration.

Risking Everything to Survive

Steve: You talked about you and Turk trading with the natives from time to time to get extra food. Since you had nothing of your own when you got to the camp, what did you have to trade?

Ernie: Well there was a bombed out factory that made cigarette paper near the camp. While the POWs on working parties were taking down the building the guards let them keep the packages of sheets of cigarette paper because they considered them worthless. We would lay them out in the sun to dry, which they did quickly, and then trim any edges scorched by the bomb blasts and fires. These were fine papers, probably Dutch top quality and made good barter for dealings with the natives for food.

Steve: Sounds like a good system.

Ernie: Not always. That's how I first got the camp record.

Steve: For trading?

Ernie: No! For standing the most strokes during a beating and joining the Black Bottom Club!

Steve: Doesn't sound like one to join.

Ernie: It's by invitation only and most of us ended up as members. The worst beating I got was seventy-five blows with something like a baseball bat on my butt for trading cigarette papers for food.

Caroline: Now you had the camp record initially.

Ernie: Yeah, but there were some British sailors in the camp as I said. We had our own building and they had their building. We never had a problem with them. One of their guys beat my record for the number of strokes from a beating, a little over two-hundred; two-hundred-ten I think before he passed out. After one-hundred the damn Jap kept telling him to fall down but he wouldn't do it. Yeah, he took it away from me. But I had seventy-five blows. Afterwards my butt was as black as that bag of yours.

Steve: What did you do to deserve that?

Ernie: I got caught trading with the natives. Actually, I had traded with the guys on the working party and the Japs caught this native merchant with a bunch of cigarette papers which nobody on the outside should have had. They beat the hell out of him and made him tell where he got the paper and he told them where he got it; from the American prisoners. So then they brought him inside of camp, lined us up at quarters and took him down the ranks picking out people who traded cigarette papers to him. He picked out four but the Jap told him he wanted one more.

Well, we were wearing hats made out of straw I guess, or bamboo, I don't know which it was. Mine was frayed around the edges as usual. The guard who was picking out people made us take our hats off. And when we did why, the merchant spotted me as one of the people that had traded with him. So they made me the head prisoner that they put in the brig I guess because it took longer to find me. They kept telling our people they were going to chop our heads off. We were in their brig for about a week of this crap and they were irregular in feeding us with even worse stuff than usual. They had always told us that the day they executed you, you'd get anything you wanted to eat and as much of it as you wanted. So that last morning, here comes a bigger, better breakfast than we had ever had and plenty of it. At noontime it was the same deal; it was more good chow. By night, well, we had lost our appetite. We were sure by then that they were going to execute us. I guess it was about 6:00 pm and we heard the commotion at the gate. The commandant was right next to the entrance of the compound. It was very close. It was a bunch of guards coming in the gate, each swinging a club and we decided it wasn't a head chopping; it was a head beating.

They had the rest of the prisoners lined up in a big field where there was like a square with the trees in the center. So they lined them up and then they took us over by the beating place and proceeded to beat the devil out of us. I was last to get it. The first, they'd take eight or ten blows and they'd fall down crying. I was too stubborn for them. I wouldn't fall down and the Japs kept telling me to fall down. I wouldn't do it. So that's when I got seventy-five licks with a ball bat, and I had a black butt.

Steve: Now who was counting? Who did the counting?

Caroline: Who counted the blows so you know how many?

Ernie: People who weren't getting beat; it sure wasn't me. If I remember right it was Turk Turner and Robbie that really did the counting.

Prison Camp Makassar's "Black Bottom Club"

Ernie:	Here's a great drawing of how it was to join the Black Bottom Club. This was drawn by a Dutch doctor, A. J. P. Borstlap, Doc Borstlap, a good artist and the man who saved my life.
Steve:	How did he do that?
Ernie:	Not yet. I thought you wanted to stay in order.
Steve:	You're right, you're right!
Ernie:	Okay then. Well, some more during this time. The worst was certainly yet to come which seems funny since I just told you about a severe beating. A lot of the guards were cruel so-and-sos but some of them seemed more like regular people. Oh, they'd still do whatever the commandant said but when no one was watching, they might be a bit human. Here's what they looked like. That one's by Doc Borstlap again.

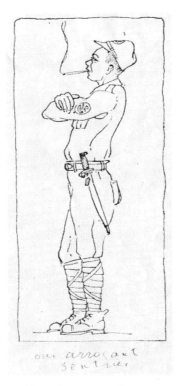

Our Arrogant Sentry

Working Around the Rules

Ernie: They usually all gave us rest periods. I think they called it "*yosabey.*" I only heard it, never saw it written so I can't help with what it means. For us it was take a break. This was probably more necessity than nice cuz in that heat if you worked without a break you'd be dead in no time. Some of the guards would try to chat with us during *yosabey*, especially since several had been educated in the States and liked to practice their English. Most times we really didn't feel like being too cozy. So one time a guard came up to me during a brake and asked me my name. I answered, "Roosevelt; I'm the president's son." He thought about that so I asked him, "What's your name?" He looked at me for a moment and said, "Tojo." Damned if that guard didn't call me Roosevelt from then on and let me call him Tojo! Tojo sort of adopted me. He would often take me along on supply runs into town to help load. He'd get me a little extra treat, like Japanese sugar candy, but Tojo said that it all had to be eaten before return to camp. Of course I always smuggled some back for my shipmates.

Steve: That sounds like a good working party to be on.

Ernie: They were few and far between. But sometimes even the hard working parties could be pleasant.

Steve: Do you have an example of that?

Ernie: Yes. So they had us build the radio station in town and then dig a trench for coaxial cable out to where these two towers were. The towers were already there, like those pillboxes were, but they had us disassemble them and move and reassemble the towers where they wanted them. Here is another Nagle original that shows step-by-step the process we went through on that job.

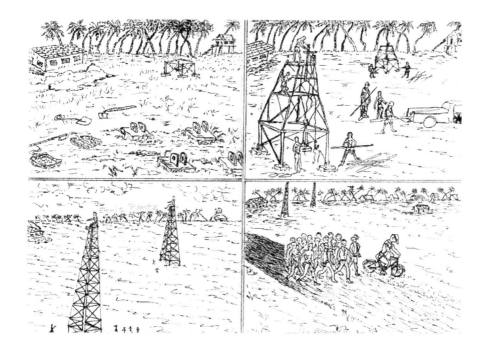

Steve:	That's really clear.
Ernie:	They were about one-hundred-fifty foot towers.
Steve:	Now I see one person on top of each tower. Are you one of these fellows on the top?
Ernie:	Yeah, I am. I liked it up there. The Japs couldn't get at me and I had a good view. I wasn't scared of falling you know. And it was like a short bit of freedom; by myself, no guards close by, nice breeze, and beautiful view.
Steve:	Like a short vacation and pleasant as long as you kept working and following the rules.
Ernie:	Right. But following the rules alone was not enough.
Steve:	How's that?
Ernie:	Sometimes you had to guess what they wanted. Or sometimes you could follow the rules blindly for a little fun. But you had to be careful.
Steve:	Can you tell me about that?

Ernie: The Japanese warrant officer in charge he wanted to take a hot bath. They liked, like I guess, a sauna or something like that, and they had a homemade one there. It was crude and they heated it with an outside fire. The warrant officer was inside this bamboo hut where the water and steam would be and he kept hollering. He had my shipmate Earl Harper feeding the doggone fire and he kept hollering at him to make it hotter. So Harper poured the wood onto the dang thing and all at once it was kind of like I guess a frog in a kettle; he was cooking him alive. The water got so hot so fast that it burned the Jap; he hopped out and then was chasing the Harper around for making his water too hot. That's what that this drawing is all about.

The Hot Bath [prisoner Harper] by Shorty Nagel

CHAPTER 9

THE DRY SEASON:
APRIL TO OCTOBER, 1944

The Years Grind On

ALTHOUGH BY THIS point Japan was obviously losing the war, the Japanese Government showed no sign of capitulation. That part of the military guarding prisoner of war camps maintained "business as usual" even as the Allied forces drew closer to the Japanese home islands. At the end of this season the battle for the liberation of the Philippines would begin and the United States' 1st Marine Division landed on Peleliu.

Steve: Okay, now we're up to the Dry Season of 1944.

Ernie: Dry was the best. We all made it through the Wet in that new bamboo camp but it was hard, hard living. Lots of guys were sick but I guess we had enough original energy left to push through. But the Dry was easier.

Steve: What kind of things went on?

Ernie: Well, still working parties, of course, but every once in a while something different would happen.

Steve: Do you have an example?

Ernie: Sure. A small group of us were sent down to do some kind of reclamation work. It was on a pier and there was a ... I think it was a ... whether it was a restaurant or some type of a fancy building I don't know. Inside that building there was a model boat; it looked like the whole thing was made of ivory for a decoration. It

85

was a beautiful thing, and on the stern were these two figurines and they had oars and they rowed the boat.

Steve: I see.

Ernie: I took the whole boat! Then I got afraid the Japs were going to find it with me. So I ditched the boat but kept the two little figurines. And I still have them, see?

Steve: Beautiful! Amazing you were able to keep them so long. Now you had to hide those?

Ernie: Oh yeah. You had to hide every damn thing you had. Yeah, you know it was pretty. Like somewhere we discovered a Sheffield kitchen knife, not a table knife, more like a carving knife. It was too big so we broke the blade off part way so it wasn't so long and sharpened it and made a razor out of it. I'm positive it was one that was really great steel because all you had to do was put it on a leather strap and you brought it up sharp like a good razor. That's what our barber used to shave all of us.

Steve: Tell me a bit more about the working parties. You would march out to the work site and work all morning but then what about lunch? Would they give you lunch at the site or would you return to camp? Or perhaps there was no lunch at all.

Ernie: Usually, the lunch was brought to us and some, a few working parties, they only worked you till noon, and then they took you back to camp. Those were shorter not because they were being nice. It was usually because it was too unbelievably hot or rainy to continue for a full day. When enough prisoners passed out they called it quits.

Steve: I see.

Ernie: But almost all the time they took one of the prisoners and a Jap guard back to the galley and picked up rations for the number of men that were on the working party.

Steve: Okay.

Ernie: It was like a wooden barrel-like thing. There was some rice in it, and then there was another container with some kind of vegetable. The Jap had a truck, so you'd take that to wherever the working party was, and then you'd have your noon hour, usually. Most of the time you got a full noon hour of rest. Again, had to because of the heat.

Caroline: There were good working parties and bad ones.

Ernie: Yeah, there were good working parties and there were bad ones, and the good ones they treated you well. A great treat was ice water, sugared ice water because it was quick, quick energy. They'd give you a container of sweetened ice water, which was really welcome in the heat.

Caroline:	Right.
Ernie:	You'd get that on a good working party. Very, very seldom the Jap would let you buy food from the native vendors that always hovered around the working party. That didn't happen very often, but sometimes it did. He'd kind of turn his head and look away, you know, let you deal with it.
Caroline:	And what did they do in the bad working party?
Ernie:	They'd whack you on the back or on the butt with a bamboo pole, just because they could, or to make you work faster, or any old excuse at all or for no reason; just to hit you. Mostly they were bad with our bodies. They were pretty sadistic. They had the same damn guards for a whole three and a half years, and if they start out beating you and mistreating you, they did that for all the time you were there.
Caroline:	How easy was it to get on a good working party?
Ernie:	Not that easy, usually just the luck of the draw. There once was an English man named Jodie Wilkinson. He was assigned to one working party that was going; the one that was not a good party to work on. But, at the same time, there was another party going up the same day that was a good one and Jody wanted to go on a good one. So he fell in as an extra man in the line for the good one at the gate. When the Japs counted you off, you know, to make sure he had the right number, he came up as an extra and they had a hell of a time identifying Jody as the extra one. Once they found him the Japs beat the hell out of him at the gate. Then they made him go in the working party anyway. It was miserable, but he brought it on himself. It was his own fault on that one. He just wanted to work for, you know, the crew where they treated you decently.
Caroline:	I can't say that I blame him. Now when would that have happened in the war?
Ernie:	This was right at the height of the Jap's power. They didn't make much difference between the beginning

88

and the end of their custody of us. The good ones were still good and the bad ones were bad right up to the end. The English, I think, took care of the bad ones in Singapore after the war. Took them to Singapore and tried them as war criminals and hung them on the spot.

Caroline: This was after the war?

Ernie: Yeah. I heard through the grapevine, you know, that that's what happened to them.

Steve: Now, back on the working parties. After the noon hour, how long would they work you for?

Ernie: Usually four o'clock. Usually until four o'clock. You'd get back into camp usually four thirty, quarter to five because most of the time you'd have to march back. Occasionally you'd be lucky to get a party that had a truck then we'd all come back in the truck.

Ernie vs. the Bees

Steve: That's what I was going to ask. Were most of these jobs within walking distance of the camp?

Ernie: Well, within three or four miles of the camp anyway: usually somewhere within the city mostly. However one time during this season we were on the wood cutting working party. They used wood to do their cooking and I guess this was about the end of the Dry. Just like here that's a good time to collect up the wood; after it's seasoned but before it gets soaked. Anyway, there was a native house there and a stream. It was an irrigation stream and very close to a native house was a great big, looked like a Beech tree and the Japanese decided that was going to be their wood but they were afraid of the tree falling on the native house. So they sent a prisoner up the tree to fasten the rope to the lowest limb so that when the tree fell it would fall away from the house; I happened to be that prisoner.

I just got pulled up to and settled on that lowest limb when a giant swarm of honey bees come pouring out of a hole. Before I could get away from them bees got me all over! I come down that damn rope in a snap and dove into the drainage ditch and drowned or at least scared off all the bees. They counted over one-hundred stings all over me and they all swelled up so much that the Japs didn't make me work anymore that day. But don't you know that was all the ill effects I ever had from it, was just swelling. It's a wonder it hadn't killed me, some people would have, I'm sure.

Steve: Right.

Ernie: I think that was one reason I could work with honey bees at home once I got out of there. They never seemed to bother me. If I got a sting, so what? Maybe that experience made me immune.

Caroline: Didn't you have bees on the farm?

Ernie: That's true. Maybe that's where I got my tolerance. Well those Java bees were just doing their job. I never held it against them.

Caroline: Was this near the house where the girl played the piano?

Ernie: I think it was.

Steve: What was that about the piano?

Ernie: There was a girl that always seemed to play her piano when the troops marched by her house, to and from working.

Steve: Okay. To entertain them? Or lighten things up?

Ernie: I think so. I don't remember what she played, whether it was "God Bless America" or something else. It was an American tune for sure.

Steve: Oh, that seems a little risky.

Ernie: Yeah, but apparently it was to brighten our spirits, and it did. I guess the guards just liked the music because they never stopped her.

Steve:	Brave girl. Now we've not talked about it but did you ever get any days off? Let's say in a typical week, would they give you any days off?
Ernie:	We did. Most of the time we got Saturday and Sunday off. Sometimes we had to work Saturday and rare occasions they'd come up with something we had to do on Sunday. But if we were off on Sunday we would hold a fishing party. Great majority of the time it was a five day week. I think the Japs liked that kind of schedule as well as we.
Caroline:	What did you do on your time off? Did you do what you wanted?
Ernie:	We washed our clothes and tried to chase the bed bugs out of our bedding.
Caroline:	Good idea.
Ernie:	And we relaxed.
Steve:	Were there lots of bugs around?
Ernie:	Yes there were. The doggone bed boards we used were from salvaged lumber. They had big old holes in them. Them bed bugs were breeding in those air holes and you couldn't get rid of them. They would hatch out and we'd kill them and more would hatch out and they just seemed to keep coming. They were bad darn it; they'd really bite you.
Caroline:	That's what you made your bed out of, right? Those boards?
Ernie:	Yeah, you had to use boards that were laying on a trestle. I guess it was about eighteen inches off the floor, about the height of a bed. These boards laid on the trestle and a *tatami* mat laid on the boards. The normal Japanese *tatami* is probably a two-inch thick woven mat but ours was a one-inch thick woven mat because that's what we got. It was better than nothing on the bare board. But the dang bed bugs would crawl through and out of that mat and on to you. About once a month we'd pick a Saturday day-off and we'd go on a bed bug fight. Everybody would bring

	their bedding and their boards out in the sun and we'd murder bed bugs. Once we got out all that we could see then we'd take them back in.
Caroline:	Did that get rid of them?
Ernie:	Temporarily. We tried plugging the holes with soap, with different stuff but they'd just eat right through it.
Caroline:	Would they let you play any sports or other entertainment?
Ernie:	No, the prisoners weren't supposed to be happy. That was the Japs' theory.
Caroline:	I see.
Ernie:	Part of your punishment of being prisoner was …
Caroline:	Not be happy.
Ernie:	Not be happy. And they damn well saw to it that we couldn't be happy.
Steve:	I know you didn't have a chaplain there but did you do anything with religious services or did somebody take charge of that?
Ernie:	You know I don't remember any religious service, don't remember anyone acting as chaplain. Maybe there was but if so I don't remember it. That didn't take place in my crew anyway.

CHAPTER 10

THE WET SEASON:
NOVEMBER 1944 TO MARCH 1945

AS THE LAST year of the war began the Japanese empire began to shrink at an increasing pace. During their last Wet Season the B-29 raids against Tokyo began, the amphibious assault of Iwo Jima occurred, and the Allies invaded Okinawa. The prisoners in Makassar experienced this only through the increasing number and intensity of bombing raids on the areas of the city around the camp by Allied planes. These attacks were both encouraging and deadly as both friend and foe were injured or killed by the indiscriminate explosives.

Second Winter in the Bamboo Camp

Ernie: The winter, the rainy season, of '44 to '45, that's when most of our people died. We had moments of relaxation and even moments of fun during that Dry Season but a lot of us had never completely shaken off the last Wet Season and we were still being slowly worked, and starved, and beaten to death. That last Wet killed a lot of men.

Caroline: Almost got you Ernie.

Ernie: Yup. It almost got me.

Steve: How did it start?

Ernie: You know, I don't exactly remember it starting. I just remember getting sicker and sicker and shivering and aching and I finally just fell down. I was spending a lot of time in the head and I was walking through the rain to the head and I never made it. My crew said I

93

	just fell facedown halfway there. Guess that was all I had in me that day.
Steve:	When did this happen?
Ernie:	I guess it was the first of January, '45 that I came down with dysentery and then on top of that malaria and I went unconscious. I was unconscious for six days. They thought I was a goner. Not many got both dysentery and malaria.
Steve:	Right.
Ernie:	They got malaria or they got dysentery, but not both.
Caroline:	And they kept moving your bed closer to the morgue. It was closer every time you woke up.
Ernie:	That was their system. I was told that one of the doctor's said I was going to die and he wasn't going to try and do anything because guys were dying eight to ten a day from the whole camp.
Steve:	Right.
Ernie:	Well I was unconscious for six days. Only when I come to, the only thing I remembered is, I remembered I talked to Jesus just as close as I'm talking to you. I'm sure it was Him.
Caroline:	What did you ask him and what did he say?
Ernie:	I asked him if I was going to die and he told me no. I was just going to be very sick. And lo and behold that's the way it played out. I wasn't a religious kid at all. Up until then I was a typical sailor: liked his drink and his women.
Caroline:	And your friends would come and visit you and afterwards you balled them out for not visiting because you didn't know it; but they had been there every day most of the day.
Ernie:	My close friends would come over to see me and I had absolutely no memory of it. They said I talked to them, but I had no memory. Once I came to and got discharged from the hospital, I jumped on them for not coming to see me while I was in bad shape. They

said "You dummy! We did see you every day." It was a funny deal. I don't remember a thing but talking to Jesus, that was it. So I've had a little experience in dealing with Him so I hope He's still thinking good towards me. If He's as good to me later as He was then, I'm in good shape. I expect He will be. I just don't know what's taking Him so long to come get me!

Caroline: What happened everyday at 3:00 pm?

The Pallbearers

Ernie: Yeah, that was the burial party and that's a drawing of it by the Doc. At 3:00 on the dot they backed an opened bodied truck up close to the barracks sickbay. They'd take the guys who had died overnight from the morgue. It was probably two-hundred feet to the truck. These guys, the pallbearers, had wooden clogs and cloaks. I can still hear those clogs going clop, clop, clop as they carried the bodies and loaded them on the truck. I can still hear it.

Yeah. And then while they were doing it they played Taps: the bugle boy played Taps. Taps is not my favorite song. I know that when I go they'll play Taps but I have told everyone that right after I want them to play Reveille!

Caroline: He said it! That's true.

Steve: How did you survive?

Ernie: Doc Borstlap.

Steve: How did he do it?

Ernie: Well when all of the others had given up on me Doc Borstlap took a try. He used a homemade needle made from I don't know what and filled it with quinine mixed with coconut juice and then shot it directly into my vein. He didn't use tap water for the injection into my vein and that's a good thing. To this day American doctors tell me that shooting coconut juice directly into my vein would kill me. It didn't. That dirty tap water probably would have but Doc Borstlap's cocktail didn't, God bless him.

Caroline: When you went for your physical down at the V.A. I remember that you told your story to the doctor and she said, "That's impossible, you'd be dead." And you said, "But I'm not!"

Ernie: I should have said "You're right, it is impossible ... that I'm not dead."

Well, after I got up and around and was recuperating from the dysentery, and the malaria, I got to ride the truck and escort these dead bodies to the local cemetery and offload them. I'm told that they built a building right over the graves of those people that were buried there because they hated the Dutch so bad. But can you imagine?

Steve: No. No I can't.

Ernie:	That's what I heard.
Steve:	What was it about that time that made everyone so sick? It seemed like that was the worst time for health. Was it just the duration of the camp, or was it a really Wet Season? Seems like a lot of people got sick and died during that time.
Ernie:	Oh, yeah it was a really Wet Season. On top of that we were all really worn out and that was our second year in that rotten bamboo camp. The year before we had better living conditions when we were in a the original camp that the Dutch had built.
Steve:	Right.
Ernie:	That camp was dry and had good ventilation. We didn't have the problem with dysentery and malaria in that camp as we did in the later camp. The later camp was built in an area that the Dutch quarantined every rainy season because it was low-lying land and really a bad place to live. That's where the Japs decided to plant us.
Caroline:	That wasn't very friendly, was it?
Ernie:	Not very, no. That's where we lost the most of our people that died ... Died living in that camp.
Caroline:	I can understand that.
Ernie:	I came so close; made it out by the skin of my teeth.
Caroline:	Yep. Your mother was praying hard.
Ernie:	Yeah I think my mother prayed me out.
Steve:	Sent you a messenger too.
Ernie:	Yeah.

Coconuts and Carabao

Ernie:	Yeah, well, when I was first out of the hospital recuperating from dysentery and malaria and my best friend, Turk Turner, was also recuperating. We had lots of coconut trees in the camp. We decided that we

would harvest some ripe nuts. We arranged it so that he climbed a tree, picked the nuts, and threw them down to me. I was to catch the damn nuts in a rattan basket to keep them from hitting the ground and thudding. We wanted to keep it quiet because it was off limits to pick the coconuts. Big trouble if you got caught. The basket was like a catcher's glove and would eliminate the momentum so that the coconut wouldn't make a noise as it would if it hit the ground. I got a few of them just fine but then I misjudged that last one and instead of it hitting in the basket, the damn thing hit my wrist and broke it. To get it set I had to go to the Jap guard who was head of the camp; Yoshida was his name. He was the head Japanese guard in camp and he owned the life or death over you. I had to go see him and show him my arm to get permission for the doctor to put a cast on it. He looked at it and he said, what the hell was it? Oh yeah: "*Crocksomo*", which was a cuss word to them. I took it to mean something like jackass.[1]

Steve: What was the word again?

Ernie: *Crocksomo.*

Caroline: What did you say that made him say that to you? What did you tell him?

Ernie: I told him I was walking outside the barracks and a Carabao charged me, knocked me down, and hit my arm. A Carabao is a water buffalo; they were big monsters but mostly tame. They took Carabao and staked them out between the barracks and let them mow the grass. Every once in a while one of them Carabao would get a thought in its head and charge someone or break loose and do some kind of damage. So it could be believable when I told the guard that the caribou charged me and knocked me down and broke my wrist. Yeah. He didn't believe what I had told more than a big fish tale, but he authorized me to go see the doctor anyway. He didn't believe me though.

	Crocksomo: jackass.
Caroline:	*Crocksomo*.
Ernie:	It's a curse word to them. Anyway that guard told the doctor to put a cast on it, which he did. I was wearing that right up until the war was over. He set it as best he could and it mostly healed but it healed crooked. It still is.
Caroline:	But then it didn't totally heal?
Ernie:	No it didn't heal. After I came back the stateside medical folks found that I had a bone fragment lodged in the joint. A Navy doctor in the States operated on it and it still wouldn't heal. There must have been some sort of prison camp crud in there that kept it raw. So finally after weeks of going to the Navy doctor, I went to a civilian doctor, and in one week he had the thing healed over. He cauterized it; it had been festering so long that it had developed a ring right around the incision so you could looked in and see the bone.
Steve:	Terrible.
Ernie:	What he did is he cauterized the thing, the flesh, with silver nitrate and then he bandaged it up and it healed over in a weeks' time. I kept avoiding the Navy doctor, but he finally did see me. He wanted to know what made it heal. I told him, I said "I went to see a real doctor." He didn't like that very well (laughs).
Caroline:	I understand that.
Ernie:	Not very diplomatic of me. Yeah, I went to see a real doctor.

Chapter 10 Notes:

1. Could have been *Kusoyarou* クソ野郎 which roughly translates Stupid Bastard.

CHAPTER 11

THE DRY SEASON:
APRIL TO AUGUST, 1945

AS THE *PERCH* men celebrated their second anniversary in captivity the long period of malnutrition combined with the deleterious effects of the swampy environs of their living quarters began to take their toll. Diseases like dysentery and malaria struck during the rains due to flooded waste systems and flourishing mosquitoes. However it was the now uncommon disease known as Pellagra that killed several of the prisoners. This is a vitamin deficiency disease most frequently caused by a chronic lack of niacin and is a symptom of malnutrition. Niacin is found in meats and fresh vegetable and nuts; few of these were routinely available to the POWs.

Fallen Friends

Steve:	I looked up some information on the six men from the *Perch* that died while in prison camp.
Ernie:	Yeah, uh huh?
Steve:	Here's what I found out. The first man is Charles Newton Brown.
Ernie:	Right. He was a kid.
Steve:	Yeah, it says here that he died April 18, 1945, so after the Wet Season. It has him and a few others dying of something called Pellagra which is a vitamin deficiency disease caused by chronic lack of vitamin B_3.
Ernie:	I never heard of that disease but I can tell you what it was: starvation. Those poor boys, and me too, was just starved down and worn out and sick and weary

	from the long Wet Season. Some just couldn't hold out any more. Their bodies swelled up and couldn't eliminate water, so it accumulated under the skin until it actually ruptured.
Steve:	I see. That's awful. Well, B_3 is niacin and it's found in tuna, chicken, turkey, and some fresh vegetables.
Ernie:	Well, we had none of that.
Steve:	No. Well Brown was a Machinist's Mate, Second Class and was from Cambridge, Massachusetts.
Ernie:	I remember him. The accent; that Boston accent.
Steve:	How about Philip James Dewes? They had him down as a warrant officer.
Ernie:	Of course. Dewes was chief pharmacist. Well, they promoted him to warrant right after the first war patrol.
Steve:	Dewes died July 25, 1945 also from Pellagra.
Ernie:	Yes. That sounds right.
Steve:	Right. Then there was Houston Ernest Edwards. He died the year before on July 10th from a combination of cerebral malaria, beriberi, and dysentery.
Ernie:	Sounds like me. That's almost the same combination I had.
Steve:	Did you know him well?
Ernie:	Yes, of course. He was a Chief Engineman. I think he was from Tennessee so we sort of had a local-boy bond.
Steve:	Now this fellow, Frank Elmer McCreary, seems to have been transferred to and died in another POW camp; it was at a Japanese POW camp in Fukuoka, Japan. Does that make sense to you?
Ernie:	I don't know, but that's right they did take the Engineman to Japan.
Steve:	Right. He was a Machinist's Mate, First Class.
Ernie:	Probably a Motor Machinist's Mate which was the same as an Engineman. They took the Enginemen to Japan, they took our Radiomen to Japan and, of

course, all the officers. I heard they put them in Ofuna, in Japan, and then from there to, you know, different working parties in Japan. Ofuna was a terrible place; like a torture chamber. It was not registered as a camp so no one knew and the Red Cross could never even complain about it.

Steve: McCreary died of pneumonia on January 4, 1943.

Ernie: That follows; torture and neglect.

Steve: Here is another shipmate that passed away on April 6, 1945: Albert Kenneth Newsome, Chief Machinist's Mate. He was another victim of the Pellagra.

Caroline: Isn't he the one that ate the poisonous berries?

Ernie: Right. He's the one that ate the pokeberries. We called them pokeberries because they looked just like them. I don't know exactly what they were.

Steve: Did he know that they were poisonous?

Ernie: Yeah. He said he didn't give a damn if he did die. Some got to that point. We were there for three years at that point; there was just no end in sight.

Steve: Why didn't you feel that hopeless?

Ernie: Maybe the hopefulness of youth!

Caroline: That's poetic!

Ernie: Well, I was still young. As I remember Newsome was an older guy; he was in his late 30s anyway. Not that that's very old but us younger guys couldn't imagine that it all wouldn't turn out okay. Maybe he was more realistic; too realistic as it turned out. And those berries might not have killed him if he wasn't so weak and malnourished already.

Steve: Right. Now one last casualty: Robert Archibald Wilson who died June 15, 1945. It looks like he was the last one to succumb.

Ernie: Yes. Wilson: Fire Controlman, First Class.

Steve: Seems like he died of bacterial dysentery and Pellagra.

Ernie: All good men. It seemed like there were all good guys on the *Perch*. And that damn camp just made them all

102

better. I don't remember anyone stealing from anyone and there was no ratting to the Japs for special treatment. Everyone hung together and if you got a little extra, you shared. It was good that way.

American Prisoners of War who have Died

1	MONK	U.S.S. "POPE"	August 9th 1942	Fireman 1st
2	GILBERT	" " POPE	December 17th 1942	Torpedo 3rd
	FRAME	" " POPE	March 23rd 1944	Radioman 2nd
	EDWARDS	" " PERCH	June 10th 1944	Chief Electr Mate
5	THORNBERG	" " POPE	January 30th 1945	Fireman 1st
	WYMAN	" " POPE	February 5th 1945	Boeswain
	SHEIDY	" " POPE	April 16th 1945	WATER TENDER 1st
8	PECK	" " POPE	March 17th 1945	Quarter Master
9	BROWN	" " ASHVILLE	March 18th 1945	Fireman 1c
10	TAWSON	" " POPE	March 11th 1945	Elof Fire boxtng
11	PARDUS	" " POPE	March 21st 1945	Seaman
12	NEWSOME	" " PERCH	April 7th 1945	Chief Machinist M
13	COLWIN	" " POPE	April 8th 1945	Yeoman 1st
14	DWYER	" " POPE	April 8th 1945	Water tender 2nd
15	GRUSH	" " POPE	April 11th 1945	Seaman 2nd
16	WILLIAMS	" " POPE	April 13th 1945	Storekeeper
17	BROWN	" " PERCH	April 18th 1945	Machinist Mate
18	SURA	" " POPE	April 18th 1945	Quarter Master 3
19	GERDES	" " POPE	March 28th 1945	Seaman 1st
20	GOOD	" " POPE	April 25th 1945	Seaman 2nd
21	HORTON	" " POPE	April 27th 1945	Seaman 1st
22	BURNS	" " POPE	April 28th 1945	Ship F 3
23	SMITH	" " POPE	April 28th 1945	Machinist

The Roll of the Dead

Signs and Rumors of the End

Steve: Now, as you said, you were held prisoner for almost three and a half years: twelve-hundred and ninety-seven days.

Ernie: That's right.

Steve: At any time were there signs that the end of the war was approaching? Some indication that you might be released in the near future?

Ernie: Well in late 1944 we began to see planes flying overhead: Allied planes. Then the allies began to really bomb the area around us at the end of 1944. They bombed the Jap warehouse section of town that was all along the harbor. One time one group of bombers, that evidently they didn't know where, bombed the wrong place; part of their bombs dropped in the camp and killed some prisoners. Part of them dropped in the camp garden where a bunch of us were working; I was working there. They near killed me.

Steve: Did you have a chance to take cover?

Ernie: I was laying in the arrowroot in the garden when it started; that was a plant about six foot tall, very dense. I was laying there; I'd come down with a malaria attack. I was laying amongst that arrowroot because a Jap told me to rest there. The planes came over and seemed like every bomb they dropped was closer to the garden. I got out of the doggone arrowroot and ran towards where the rest of the guys were and then dropped down in a drainage ditch. Around the garden was a drainage ditch that was dry and that's where we laid flat. It wasn't very deep but you don't know how close you can hug the ground when something like that's happening. One bomb sure did scare the hell out of us. We were trying to get deeper in the ditch and the B-29s came over and let loose. One bomb went off pretty close and even though I was as low in that trench as I could get a piece of shrapnel came whizzing by and cut my doggone pants! I had just drawstring pants and that was all; it cut my pants but didn't cut the skin, just cut the butt of my pants because I couldn't get it low enough and that's what was sticking out; my skinny little butt. It's funny now but that was a scary, scary raid.

Steve: Who was doing the bombing?

Ernie: They didn't stop and say hello. But they did almost kill me.

Steve: No doubt. Weren't there any shelters you could go to during aid raids? You would think that the methodical guards would have considered that.

Ernie: There were slit trenches all over the place that we had made. There were real shelters in the center of camp and trenches toward the outer areas.

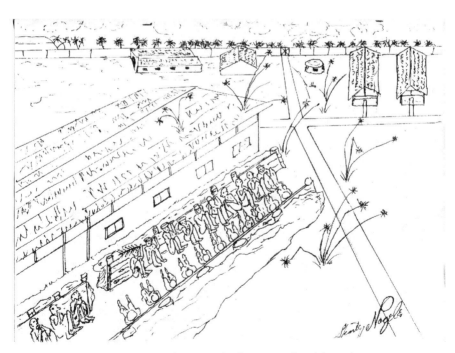

Prisoners in a slit trench during Allied bombing

Ernie:	When the Japs saw the bombing coming they always took us back to camp. This time the bombing came too quick for them to get us assembled and headed to camp, so we just had to do what we could to protect ourselves in the location we happened to be in, in the garden. There were shelters and you were required to go into them during an air raid. We were just caught too far away from one that time.
Steve:	What were these shelters like?
Ernie:	I'm sure there's a drawing of one. Oh, here it is. That's right; we called them rabbit-holes, *konynenhol* in Dutch. They worked pretty well; they should since they were American made. Of course nothing can take a direct hit but a least the shrapnel wouldn't get you.
Steve:	It looks like a little mine.
Ernie:	Something like that. Rabbit-hole.
Steve:	So you were required to go there during a raid?
Ernie:	Yes. The Japs had sirens, just like us, and when they sounded all the rabbits had to go in their holes. By the summer of 1945 it seemed like we had more air raids than not. Of course every time a plane flew over they would sound the alarm and down the hole we were supposed to go.
Steve:	They were American planes you think?
Ernie:	Probably so. Japs didn't have any planes left by that time. They were the Allies; the Americans, I think.
Caroline:	They were bombing because they didn't know you were there, did they?
Ernie:	No, they did not know we were there. The Japanese probably never told them they had a camp of prisoners there. They never called us prisoners; they called us hostages. Now what kind of sense that makes I do not know.
Caroline:	Right.

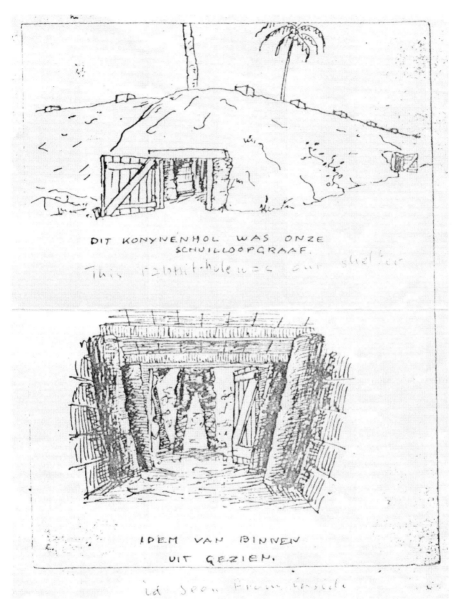

Views of "The Rabbitholes"

Ernie:	We had one curious British sailor that got killed during a bombing raid. He got out of the bomb shelter because he wanted to see what was going on. He saw it.
Caroline:	He found out the hard way.
Ernie:	Yeah, uh-uh. That was a needless one. Americans are smarter than that. Once you had your britches cut by shrapnel, you're leery of those bombs.
Steve:	Yeah, that's too close for comfort, right?
Ernie:	Too close for comfort is right.
Steve:	Did you always go into the shelter?
Ernie:	Funny you should ask that because no, I did not. As it got later in the year the raids became more frequent. I got sick of getting rousted out of my rack by the Jap guard. He would come in the barracks and whack each bunk with his stick to make sure everyone was out. It was dark but if you were in your bunk then 'whack' on the butt or wherever and off you'd go to the shelter probably with a few more whacks.
Steve:	How did you avoid that?
Ernie:	I'd sleep under my bunk. If you remember the base of the bed, the boards, were supported by a trestle about two feet off the ground. I'd get my *tatami* or whatever and just crawl under my bed and sleep there. They couldn't see me so I didn't have to go. I fooled myself into thinking I was safe but really a nearby bomb explosion probably would have killed me.
Caroline:	The blissful ignorance of youth.
Ernie:	Exactly.

CHAPTER 12

LIBERATION

WITH THE LOSS of Iwo Jima and Okinawa in early 1945, both considered part of the "home" islands, the Japanese began to realize the inevitability of ultimate defeat. The activities of the American submarine force combined with the mining of Japanese harbors effectively ended their merchant shipping; Japan had been deprived of the raw materials necessary for continued war activities. Though by August even their few remaining naval vessels that remained operational could not operate due to extreme lack of fuel, they remained defiant. Only the detonation of the atomic bombs on Hiroshima on August 6 and Nagasaki on August 9 forced capitulation on August 15 by Emperor Hirohito.

The Long Night Ends

Steve: Now how long were you in the camp? When did you finally get out?

Ernie: 1,297 days. That's three and a half years if you convert it. It was from March 3, 1942 to September the 18th, 1945.

Steve: When we talked before I think you said that it was around August the 15th when you found out or you were told the war was over.

Ernie: Yes, that sounds right. We had started out on working parties but about 10:00 the Japs started to bring us back to camp and we wondered why. It was because they had surrendered to the Americans. They assembled us all in the afternoon if I remember right, and

109

they read from a piece of paper that said that Japan had surrendered to the Americans. The reader also said that now we were all friends. Can you imagine? They wanted to shake hands! Believe me, we didn't think too much about shaking hands with them. These were the same guys who beat the hell out of you for three and a half years and now you're friends? These were the same bastards that beat us and starved us for three and a half years, because we kept the same guards from beginning to end. They wanted to shake hands and be friends. Needless to say, nobody did. Actually I guess they really meant it because in retrospect, they've been pretty good friends of ours since then. Ever since the war they've always been on our side. Anyway, all that friendship was off in the future and we had no feeling about being friends with our torturers.

Steve: No. I can't imagine you would. Was there any retaliation against the guards?

Ernie: You know, I can't remember even one time that anyone took it out on them. They deserved it, make no mistake. But we didn't dole it out. Maybe we were too weak or just too glad to have made it through. I don't know but it didn't happen.

Caroline: That's amazing.

Steve: So what did you do differently after the announcement that the war was over?

Ernie: Well the English took over the handling of the Japs who were now the prisoners in the beginning when the war was ended. They took the Japs and made them turn in their weapons to a weapons barn. And then, they locked them up. You know I wanted to bring a Jap weapon back with me, as a souvenir you know, after we got released. They were in our custody in that weapons barn. So I went and I told the British guard that I wanted a gun. He took me right inside and I picked out the side-arm that I wore after that. It

110

looked good to me and made me feel good too. It was a Japanese pistol that looked like a Luger. It was a beautiful gun with a polished holster and the whole fancy bit. I was proudly wearing that damned thing but when we hit Borneo the American troops there took it away from me. I'm convinced that some dog-gone American G. I. brought that thing home with him.

Steve: What a shame.

Ernie: He took it away and made me turn it in. It was a beautiful gun.

Steve: It took them a while to come and get you, didn't it?

Ernie: Well they didn't know we were there.

Steve: So, if I understand you, the war is over but the Americans didn't know you were on that island?

Ernie: That's right. The Americans did not know that we were even alive. Nobody knew. At least they thought the *Perch* men were all dead. Sunk.

Steve: So how did they find out that you were alive in Makassar?

Ernie: So we had to make emergency contact with them with a jerry-built radio transmitter that one of the guys did. We had a radio striker in camp. He got a hold of a radio, a regular radio that he cobbled together with some other parts and made a transmitter out of that and sent a message. Pretty ingenious; just a regular radio and a bunch of other radio parts. From that the message got out. Somebody with the Allies copied that and they said they'd investigate and lo and behold, there we were. Then they flew an American Air Force general, a major general, in to look over the camp, take pictures, and survey. What a sight for him I imagine! And finally they flew in planes to evacuate us to Borneo. It looked like one of those flying boats, those twin-engine flying boats, called a PBY. I was never so glad to see anyone as I was to see that American Flier that had landed and come to rescue us. But

111

	they could only haul ten or twelve at a time so it took them lots and lots of trips to get us all out.
Steve:	Do you know about how many men there were in the camp?
Ernie:	Well originally there were about three thousand. But I think when the war was over there was about, oh, less than a thousand. And that was made up of us Americans plus some English, Dutch, and Australians and there were a few Indonesians as prisoners; ones who wouldn't go along.
Steve:	How did the population drop so dramatically? Was that mostly through death that the number of men decreased or was it through transfer?
Ernie:	Mostly through death but not that high a percentage of Americans died. They were tougher. The English and the Dutch were probably the fastest to go.
Caroline:	Especially the British Boy Sailors.
Steve:	What were those?
Ernie:	Young sailors but they didn't have that many of them. The English had a system back then of enlisting young boy sailors. If they were twelve years old they could enlist until they're eighteen. And when they turned eighteen, if they wanted to make a career out of the Navy then they could ship in as a regular able bodied seaman. We had a number of them that were prisoners that had been on an English battleship. They'd get sick and when those guys were dying they'd lay there all night long crying for their mothers. Broke your heart. I don't think any of them made it out.
Steve:	Now where did they take you first once you were liberated?
Steve:	To Borneo?
Ernie:	Yeah. They sent us to Borneo and had more troops there. The Japanese soldiers were settled in a camp surrounded by barbed wire there. The American guards offered us the opportunity to go in and beat the hell out of one, or shoot one, or do whatever we

112

	wanted to. But we didn't take them up on that offer. I guess that was good for us. We hated individual guards but we didn't hate the Japanese as a group.
Steve:	Those other Americans on Borneo, what was their reaction to you people because you were all very skinny at that point.
Ernie:	Yeah. Maybe that's why they offered to let us kill some Japs. We were skinny as skeletons. Really walking bones. My weight had dropped down to somewhere between seventy-five and eighty pounds while I was unconscious I guess. I don't know what I weighed when I got sick but I suspect about a hundred and ten, probably, because I weighed a hundred and seventy-five when the Japs got me.
Steve:	It doesn't seem possible.
Ernie:	I just slowly lost weight, you know, over three and a half years. Then when I got sick there was nothing to fall back on. I remember I could reach around my damn leg with one hand. You see pictures of starving people? That was us; we were frighteningly skinny.
Steve:	Did they do anything special for you guys?
Ernie:	I remember that they wanted to put a little weight on us in the worst way because we were so skinny. They started to make special meals for us. Funny thing is that we were plenty hungry enough but we couldn't eat hardly anything. Our stomachs had shrunk to the point that they wouldn't hold much but those guys ordered up for us anyway. They put steak and eggs in front of us and we couldn't eat much of it at all. A few bites of that feast and you were done!
Steve:	Did anybody get sick trying to eat it?
Ernie:	I don't remember anyone getting sick over that. They may have but I don't remember it.
Steve:	I only ask because I've read some Army reports of the liberation of Nazi concentration camps. The American liberators had to be very careful of what they fed those poor people at first because good food with a lot

113

of fat in it actually hurt them since they were used to so few calories and no fat. A few even died from the experience; they were that weak. So they started over with tiny meals and just gradually increased the size and content very cautiously and deliberately until they were more back to normal.

Ernie: Me, too. Same for our people too. They tried to control what they gave us. The thing is however, I guess we were eating as much rice as we wanted. That didn't seem to hurt anyone.

Steve: How about now? Do you eat rice now?

Ernie: Oh, yeah, I like rice pudding but I'm not as much for plain rice. I've always liked rice pudding though.

Steve: I thought maybe you had so much of it then, you just couldn't stand it.

Ernie: For a while I couldn't. After I got out, none, then slowly I went back to where I would eat rice. But for a number of years I couldn't stand the looks or smell of it.

Caroline: Now how did you get back to the States?

Ernie: Flew back. They gave us a choice once we got to the Philippines, I think it was about ten days in the Philippines while we stayed and got organized. They also continued to try to put a little weight on us; we were still so skinny. Then they gave us a choice. We could go back by ship, go west and go through the Suez Canal and back to New York or we could fly east back across the Pacific to San Francisco. So, some of the guys chose to go by ship but some of us chose to go by plane. I chose plane. So they flew us back. Those that had made it.

Caroline: Those that had made it?

Ernie: There was fifty-nine total, counting the officers that went into the water when the *Perch* went down for the last time; all but six survived. Six died in the prison camps and they mostly died in 1945; in the last blasted six months.

114

Back in the States

Steve: So you flew out of the Philippines. Where did you go first?

Ernie: If I remember right, I got a ride out of Manila on a bomber that was heading to Pearl; the base at Pearl Harbor. Of course they didn't have any passenger seats for people to sit on, so there was a group of us that sat in the cargo hold. Not much in the way of comfort but I was damn glad to be able to be heading home.

Steve: You made it back to Pearl.

Ernie: Right, and at Pearl they did recognize that we were special people; I'm sure now that notification had gone out ahead of us. An officer met us at the airport where we landed and then he stayed with us all the time we were in Pearl. We were there for, I don't know - five, six days. I don't remember exactly how many days. But they escorted us everywhere; they took us to the Navy Exchange and let us buy anything we wanted there that was on display. I say buy but we didn't have to buy, they gave it to us. I chose a watch. Other people chose different things, but I wanted a watch. I remember to this day it was a Timex.

Steve: Where did you go next?

Ernie: After that week they flew us from Pearl to a military hospital in Oak Knoll, California. The treatment there wasn't so special. We had to recognize that in that place, Oak Knoll, we were one of many. There were lots of battle injured men and we were just men with a different kind of injury. Course, I think now that us ex-prisoners were probably all badly wounded; just that those wounds didn't show. Anyway, Pearl was the best treatment of all.

Caroline: They call that PTSD.

Ernie: You're right but we didn't call it anything then. They know better now.

Steve:	Now how long did they give you at Oak Knoll to rehabilitate, if you will?
Ernie:	They were trying to fatten us up I believe. They didn't tell us that, but I think that's what they were doing. We were still mostly like skeletons. I really don't recall any treatment other than increased diet.
Steve:	Right. How long were you there?
Ernie:	Well they gave me initially ninety days leave and they told me if I needed more to call them and they'd give me a thirty day extension. Naturally I needed more so they gave me a thirty day extension, so about four months.
Steve:	Of the *Perch* men, did everyone who survived the camp, did they all recover and get most of their health back?
Ernie:	The rest of us mostly recovered. Some of them died fairly soon after they got out of camp for one reason or another. There's one that lived in Tennessee that - he stepped off the curb right after he arrived in his hometown and got hit by an automobile, never even got home after all of that. I can't remember his name.
Steve:	He was a *Perch* man?
Ernie:	Yes but I don't remember what his name was. Our captain didn't survive the year either.
Steve:	Was that Captain Hurt?
Ernie:	Yes. He was killed in a hunting accident on November 23rd of that same year. I've often wondered if it was an accident. I hope it was just that and not something else. He was a great guy. Like a father to a lot of us, officers and enlisted.
Steve:	You guys had a lot of awful experiences to carry around with you.
Ernie:	Yes; true. Well that might explain why the first thing we wanted to do when we got back to the States after eating was drink; in fact, mostly drink. At Oak Knoll they gave us liberty almost all the time. If you didn't

have a doctor's appointment or some medical test you were on liberty. Well, we wanted to go to San Francisco and that's what, fifteen miles maybe from Oak Knoll to San Francisco? So we decided to make it interesting. We would start walking from the hospital in the direction of San Francisco and stop at each bar along the way and have one drink. We tried for three or four days in a row. We never did get to San Francisco but we sure did get drunk. Yup. I don't think we made it even one time but we did try!

Caroline: You were persistent.

Ernie: That we were.

Operator 5

Ernie: After that initial time at Oak Knoll we were transferred to the U. S. Naval Hospital at Great Lakes in Illinois. I spent almost a full year there from about October 1945 to September 1946.

Caroline: You were getting over those three and a half years.

Ernie: That is true. Recuperating and getting medical treatment. Me for my arm of course and the other guys had different little things wrong with them. And, but then in the blasted hospital, they just about turned you loose because we'd come back Monday morning from a weekend liberty and go to sick call and the doctor would check on how you were doing and then at four o'clock that evening they'd grant us liberty again. So you wouldn't have to be back until next Monday. There were four of us that traveled all around together; it was me, Robbie, Winger, and Arts. We were like the Four Musketeers instead of Three Musketeers.

[L to R] Ernie Plantz, Winger, Robison 1946

Steve:	So just really check in once a week?
Ernie:	Yeah.
Caroline:	No wonder your wrist didn't heal.
Steve:	It was getting all that exercise. Overuse.
Caroline:	And he's right handed too!

Ernie, Robison, and Winger family at Council Bluffs

Ernie: I know. One weekend we'd go to my home in Ohio
            and one weekend we'd go to Robbie's home in Ken-
            tucky and the following weekend we'd go to Winger's
            home in Iowa, Keosauqua, Iowa. We stopped at Arts'
            home in Ohio too. So anyway we did lots of traveling,
            and drinking.

Steve: Sailors love to drink.

Ernie:	Yeah, I remember on *Perch*, the Engineer was a stickler. When it was working time, it was working time; he expected you to be working, no matter what. Our Chief Electrician, guy by the name of Edwards, came back early in the morning after all-night drinking in the Philippines before the war. He couldn't get in his bunk in the after torpedo room, so he crawled underneath the bunk. Chief Engineer came back making his tour through the boat and here's these feet sticking out from under the bunk. And he said "Who's down there?" "Edwards sir" was the reply. "What are you doing Edwards?" the Engineer asked. Edwards said "Sir I'm gonna find that goddamned dime if it's the last thing I ever do!"
Caroline:	Quick thinking.
Ernie:	I'll always remember that. Poor Edwards. A good, decent guy.
Caroline:	That's pretty good. But why Poor Edwards?
Ernie:	He was one of the ones that died in the camp.
Caroline:	Oh!
Ernie:	Anyway, you know each time I'd get back to the hospital there'd be a message to call Operator 5 in Athens, Ohio. Well I didn't know anyone in Athens, Ohio. The heck with it, it's more fun to drink. So I'd just ignore that call from Operator 5. So when they finally sent me on leave from the hospital, I don't know what possessed me but I bought my train ticket to Athens, Ohio. I thought "Well, I'll surprise the folks." First I went to the Post Office to get their address. They didn't have any record of anyone by that name so the postman and I went to the Chief of Police. He didn't have any records either so the three of us went to the Mayor's office. Pretty soon I had the postman, the Mayor, and the Chief of Police all trying to find my parents. Later on I'm hold up in a hotel when it dawned on me; you're in Athens, why don't you call that Operator 5? So I called up and asked for

Operator 5 and she says "Where you at?" I says, "I'm right here in Athens in a hotel." She says, "Stay right there, don't go away," she says, "I'll get your dad on the phone." So she called him. Well Dad didn't have a phone, so there was a black fellow about, oh, half a mile I guess from where they lived that ran a little store and a gas station. He had the phone. So the operator called him because he was the contact for all the neighbors around him. That nice man ran all the way up to my parent's house to tell Dad that his son was back from the dead. Dad and the store man got in the old truck and drove down to the phone and the operator connected Dad and me. You will have to imagine what we said. After a while I asked him "Where the heck you at?" He say, "Oh I'm down Middleport, Pomeroy way." I says, "Where's that?" He says, "It's about twenty-five miles south from Athens. I'll come get you." I says, "What are you driving?" He says, "A beat up old dump truck." I says, "Better yet, I'll just rent me a taxi." So I rented a taxi and he gave me the address and away we went. Let's see, I think it would be better if I make arrangements, so I got a taxi that took me home. I didn't know whether Dad would make it with that old dump truck or not. Anyway, I took a taxi home. Needless to say, people were glad to see me. My sister Garnet came from West Virginia and she was almost there by the time I got down home. I don't know that she must have flown that old car of theirs. They had a little Ford coupe, my sister and brother-in-law did. He was in a hospital in Indiana. He got shot in France in the landing over there. So my sister was alone, she and her baby; my niece really.

Some of my family: Maxine Darst, J. M. Plantz, Sadie and
Cash Darst, and Grandpa Joe Hill.

Ernie and Norma; reunited.

Caroline:	And when you went back home didn't you go visit your junior high or high school?
Ernie:	High School. South Charleston High School, South Charleston, West Virginia. They had me listed as 'Presumed Dead' and in the city they had a hero board with the names of the war dead from the area and my name was on that. So first I went to the high school and visited the principal. It was on Assembly Day so he had me talk to all the students. I wanted to see my science teacher because he had always been one of my favorite teachers. He had been promoted to principal of the junior high school in the city. When I walked into his office he looked at me and he turned just as white as a doggone sheet. He says, "Ernie Plantz, you're dead! What are you doing here?" I say, "They forgot to tell me!" Oh Lordy! Good old Mr. Poe.
Caroline:	It must have been something for your parents to have no word for all that time and then have you show up. It's amazing that they didn't have a heart attack or something.
Ernie:	A lot of homecomings were the same way.
Steve:	Maybe your phone call saved them; it gave them a chance to get used to the idea.
Caroline:	For five minutes or so, yeah. It's a miracle they survived the shock!
Ernie:	I'm glad they did. All good people. You know, for example, during my trip back to South Charleston, I stopped there at a drugstore for something. I don't remember what it was now. I pulled my wallet out and I ended up leaving the thing laying on the counter. It had over $900 in it.
Steve:	That's a lot of money.
Ernie:	Yeah. Well I called the store and, you know, told them what I had done and they said "Don't worry about it. We'll take care of it until you come back." So the next time I went back I went to the drugstore and they gave me my wallet, with all the money and everything inside was still good; not a penny was missing. I don't know if you could do that today or not; good people.

123

CHAPTER 13

BACK TO NORMAL

Rejoining the Submarine Fleet

Steve: Well, once you finished recuperating at the hospital where did you go next?

Ernie: I ended up on a boat at Great Lakes, Illinois but I did a number of small jobs first. I think they were trying to reward me for my hard times by giving me what they thought were fun and easy jobs.

Caroline: What kind of jobs?

Ernie: Oh, various. But I was a chauffeur at the United Nations for a short while.

Steve: In New York City?

Ernie: Yeah. Yeah, that was in late '46, and January of '47. I was in that damn hospital for almost ten months.

Steve: Why was that so long?

Ernie: That was because of my durn wrist.

Caroline: Right.

Ernie: It broke, by that coconut of course, and it healed crooked. They fooled around with that damn thing and finally removed a bone fragment, but then the darn thing wouldn't heal from the nasty wound. Also, I wasn't around much so they seemed in no rush to get rid of me. And I was doing my best to support the local economy!

Caroline: Oh brother!

Ernie: That's right. Anyway they finally sent me to New York where I chauffeured for a diplomat from South Africa. It was their Prime Minister.

Caroline:	That's when you lost the car, right?
Ernie:	That's right.
Steve:	This is the chauffeur car? You lost the limousine?
Ernie:	Yeah, well I was doing my driving job and, it was a Ford if I remember, and I dropped off my passenger. On the way back to camp I stopped at a White Castle to get me something to eat. I don't think I was in there over five minutes and looked outside and didn't have a car; it was gone! Somebody swiped it!
Caroline:	All gone.
Ernie:	Right. Anyway, the car was gone and my swearing wouldn't bring it back so I went back up to City College, which is where we were living at the time, and reported it to the colonel by the name of Corn. He was a marine colonel.
Steve:	How do you spell that last name?
Ernie:	Corn as far as remember. Colonel Corn; how's that for a name?
Steve:	Difficult to say with a straight face!
Ernie:	You got that. Well, he says well, he says do two things. He says go down to the police station and report the car stolen and he says you come back and you put yourself on report. "You won't be driving again" that colonel said.
Steve:	So that was the end of your driving?
Ernie:	Well I worked changing flat tires for a while but I was, at the time, pretty thick with a lady who worked in the Prime Minister's office. Mickey Rooney was her name; I think it was actually Michelle but everyone called her Mickey. Anyway, when I reported to her what had happened and she relayed the word eventually up to the Prime Minister; Jan Christiaan Smuts was his name. Smuts told her not to worry that he would have the detail's Executive Officer take care of it. The Exec called Colonel Corn and wanted to know where his special driver was; that was me. The colonel told him that I was working with the Motor Pool. Well the Exec kept on and wanted to know when I

would be back driving. Colonel Corn said "He won't be back driving; he's lost a car and he's got a court-martial coming up. He can't drive again." Didn't that Exec say "I'll have the Prime Minister check with Washington and see why not!" That Marine colonel backed right down and told him "Never mind. He'll be back tomorrow." So the charges were dropped.

Steve: It's good to know the right people.

Ernie: Yes it is. That crazy Smuts! Well Colonel Corn called me in immediately to give me the word. He said "I don't know who you know or how you did it but you're going back driving tomorrow." He says, "Don't try this again! I warn you; if you have any more trouble, you'll be in real trouble with me." I kept my eye on my car and had no problems with the colonel. That was my first education in the importance of who you know.

Steve: Your riders name was John Christian?

Ernie: Jan Christiaan Smuts. He was a military man as well as the prime minister of South Africa at the time. A kind fellow.

Jan Smuts
Dutch National Archives, The Hague, Fotocollectie Algemeen Nederlands Persbureau (ANEFO), 1945-1989 bekijk toegang 2.24.01.04 Bestanddeelnummer 902-2098

Steve: Okay. How about right after that? Where did you go next?

Ernie: Well I wanted to go back to the boats and I asked to go back. I guess someone figured out that my style was more suited to that than to diplomacy so I got assignment to the reserve submarine, the *Tautog* (SS199). They sent me to Portsmouth, New Hampshire and we put it in what was called Reserve Commission and then I rode her under tow from Portsmouth down to New Orleans. There was a paddle-wheel boat and a floating dry-dock there. They put the Tautog up in this thing, this floating dry-dock and then the paddle-wheel boat pushed us up the river from New Orleans to the Illinois Canal. Then they off loaded us there into the canal and they pulled her through the canal up to Chicago, which really became the Illinois River. When they got to Chicago they reinstalled our shears and periscopes, you know, the stuff that they had to remove because it wouldn't pass under the bridges through the canal. Then they towed us across to Milwaukee and berthed her right in downtown Milwaukee.

I stayed there for two years as ship's keeper and instructor; that was good duty! It was probably the best duty I could possibly have had after the war. Because of my time in service and rate I went from second class to chief electrician, you know, when I went back to duty. But I sure as hell didn't know what a chief electrician is supposed to know. I also don't think I remembered the submarine quite as well as I should have. I knew the *Perch* well enough but by this time I had been away from boats for almost five years. So by teaching the reserves it gave me a good opportunity to learn myself what I didn't know, or at least relearn it. So it helped a heck of a lot when I went to an operating boat later on. Here I am topside on the *Tautog*; I look a lot healthier for sure. I think this is the summer of 1948. I was there from April of '47 till June of '49.

USS *Tautog*, Ernie on left, "Low Pressure" Brown on right

Caroline:	Now a lot of your *Perch* buddies got out of the Navy.
Ernie:	Yeah, the majority of them did really. They wanted to go home. I wanted to stay; the Navy was my home at that time.
Steve:	So what kind of assignments did you have after the *Tautog*? You were in the Navy for thirty years, right?
Ernie:	Thirty years, four months and ten days. Take a look at that plaque on the wall.
Steve:	Oh. Perfect! This lists all of your commands.
Ernie:	I keep it up there so I don't have to keep it in my head.
Steve:	Yes; convenient. Okay, so let me go through them with you.
Ernie:	Okay.
Steve:	So first off we have Ninth Naval District Great Lakes; January 1947 to April 1947. Okay, then your time on the *Tautog*. Then after that was the *Diablo*?

Ernie:	Yes. June '49 to January '50. That was my first real sea duty.
Steve:	Okay. Where was that out of?
Ernie:	That was down in Norfolk. Yeah.
Steve:	Norfolk. What were you? You were chief on board?
Ernie:	I was Chief Electrician, yeah. I was the second chief electrician they had.
Steve:	Okay.
Ernie:	And when they needed to transfer a chief to Groton I was the one they transferred, kicking and screaming all the way.
Steve:	Oh. Did you like the *Diablo*?
Ernie:	Yes. Very much.
Steve:	Then you went to Atlantic Reserve Fleet?
Ernie:	Yeah. The reserve fleet. We reactivated submarines. I think it was thirteen boats that we put back in commission. My job, of course, was electrical. We'd have to go throughout the boat and get it all back in shape. We got all those boats ready to go to Korea.
Steve:	Right. That was April 1951 to February 1954.
Ernie:	Right, uh huh (affirmative).
Steve:	Then you went to the *Spikefish* from February 1954 to March 1961. Whoa, long time!
Ernie:	Right, uh huh. That was my last boat. I was the Chief of the Boat (COB).
Steve:	I see. Very good. Now I know you became an officer at some point. When did that happen?
Ernie:	On the *Spikefish* at the end of my time onboard. I got a commission from there. The way that happened was that my captain told me he was going to recommend me for a commission. At the time I was the COB and happy as a clam so I told him, "I don't want to. I've got orders for shore duty. My last tour. I'm going to Phoenix, Arizona." He said "Well Chief, I'm going to put you in for commission and you're going to take it." I says "What makes you so damn sure I'm going

to take it?" He says "Because if you don't, I'm going to kick your ass so high you have to take your shirt off to take a crap." I says "Well if you put it that way, I guess I'll take it." Much to my surprise, I made it. I had nothing to do with it. He just recommended me. I had nothing to do with it.

Steve: You were eight years on the *Spikefish*? Then you went to *Bushnell*?

Ernie: Right, that's a tender, submarine tender at Key West.

Steve: Key West? That sounds fun.

Ernie: In between the *Spikefish* and the tender, I went to Officer's Candidate School up in Newport.

Steve: Okay. I see the gap here, March to May 1961.

Ernie: Yeah.

Steve: Newport and Key West, all the terrible locations, huh?

Caroline: Pretty hard to take.

Steve: What was your job on the *Bushnell*?

Ernie: I was the electrical officer. That was my first tour on there, electrical officer.

Families and families:
A dark night but a brighter dawn

Ernie: That was a good tour I think.

Caroline: Yeah but the first time you were on the *Bushnell*, what tragic thing happened to you the first time?

Ernie: Oh, Carolyn, my first wife, yeah that's true.

Caroline: That was pretty tragic.

Ernie: There was a boating accident. We were out fishing and minding our own business and one of those gulf coast shrimp boats, about 45 - 50 ton, ran us down. Yeah and she went out one side of the boat, I went out the other. The side she went out pulled her right into the screw. Almost cut her leg off, it was a horrible mess.

Steve:	That's awful!
Ernie:	We changed sides just before the collision. It was odd because of the side of my boat that she was on when the collision came, and I don't know why, but we had just changed sides. I can't figure that one out at all, unless it was the Lord's way of protecting me. I just don't know.
Caroline:	He must have figured that you could support the family.
Ernie:	That's the only thing I can figure. Because I can't figure it out any other way.
Caroline:	I know. This left you with three little kids. The youngest was two-and-a-half.
Ernie:	Yep.
Steve:	Was it just you two on the boat that got run down?
Ernie:	No. Her aunt and uncle were there on the boat too. They wanted to go fishing. We were on a seventeen foot fiberglass boat. Normally, I would have gone out with her uncle alone but for whatever reason, when we decided to go, my wife said, "I'm going too."
Caroline:	Didn't you say the girls had just had chicken pox and you'd been out to sea and you just came back from sea? She probably wanted some time off.
Ernie:	Yeah. She said a strange thing just before we left. She told Linda, the oldest daughter, that she was going out fishing and she told her to take care of her little brother. Like she knew she wasn't coming back.
Caroline:	Makes you wonder.
Ernie:	Yeah, makes you wonder.
Caroline:	Yep. Anyway, that was not a good time on the *Bushnell*.
Ernie:	Not a good time, you're right.
Caroline:	Ernie used to have nightmares.
Ernie:	Yep. Not a good one.
Caroline:	Asking, "Why?" I don't have an answer but it must have been God's plan.

Steve:	I see. Then you went from September of '64 to May '65 to the Sub base up here in New London?
Ernie:	I was at the sub base in New London at submarine school.
Steve:	And then *Bushnell*, again, was it still down in Key West?
Ernie:	Back to *Bushnell* then, as Chief Engineer.
Steve:	Chief Engineer?
Ernie:	Yeah. Rough start to that tour. I didn't have to relieve somebody; they didn't have an Engineer so I just assumed the job. Two weeks later we had a big fire in the engine room. They tried to hang me for it. Fortunately, I had friends in good places that said, "Hey no, it didn't happen that way."
Steve:	That's good.
Caroline:	There was a question whether the CO would let you come back north to get married.
Ernie:	That's true. It was only a slight one.
Caroline:	I was relieved when you got off the plane.
Ernie:	That was September 1965.
Caroline:	Then you came back to sub school?
Ernie:	Right.
Steve:	Now when did you two meet? How did you start seeing each other?
Caroline:	I answered the telephone.
Steve:	You answered the telephone?
Caroline:	I answered the telephone. That's how we met. You want to tell Steve? He wondered how we met and I said, "I answered the telephone."
Ernie:	She answered the telephone. It's true. I had met an acquaintance of hers. I won't call her a friend, because I don't think she really was, at a party. I was going to take her home. I met this gal at a sub school party. I ended up taking her home and then we had no further contact until about a month later. The Submarine Birthday Ball was coming up and I was looking for a

	date. I called her and she said, "I'd love to but I've gotten engaged since I met you." She said, "I don't think he'd like it." I said, "Well, I won't tell him."
Caroline:	Continue.
Ernie:	Yeah okay, so I says to her, I says, "Do you happen to know of another lady that might like to go?" I don't think she hesitated fifteen seconds till she said "Yes, I do." She gave me Caroline's name and she says, "You wait I'll call her and tell her you're an alright guy she can safely go with you." This was in the morning time and I waited all day, pretty impatient with myself. Finally I called Caroline and told her who I was and how many kids I had and my whole life history.
Caroline:	You'd been in the Navy for years and years and you were only a Lieutenant.
Ernie:	Finally, I got around to asking her if she'd like to go to the birthday ball with me as my date. She didn't hesitate. She said "I would love to but I need to meet you before." So I went to the meeting at her house and she had her mother there and a friend of hers that was a school teacher in Groton. They looked me over; I don't know if Caroline wasn't too impressed. She thought she'd give me to her mother.
Caroline:	I did.
Ernie:	But she did agree to go to the birthday ball with me. This is what my intent was.
Steve:	That was like a panel interview, right?
Caroline:	Right because I couldn't stand him and he couldn't stand me. I can hear my father from up above who said, "You made a commitment unless there's some dire reason, you have to keep it." Because I didn't like him, and he didn't like me. Yet we had already said we would go to the birthday ball. Continue dear.
Ernie:	My boss was a Lieutenant Commander named Warren Kelley. He was going to go and at the last minute he backed out because his date found a better catch than him.

134

Caroline:	He was a widower with three kids also.
Ernie:	He said "I'm not going to go." I said, "I know a good looking gal that might be willing to be your date if you'd like." He agreed. I contacted Caroline and she did the checking for me and Marilyn, the good looking girl, said "Why not?"
Ernie:	I was a pretty good date I understand.
Caroline:	You were. Ernie's friend was off schmoozing, going around to meet the right people. Ernie had both of us girls as dates and he was very attentive. Marilyn and I decided that we could go out with these guys for fun. We were teachers and had a classroom of kids so we didn't need any more kids but we would go out with them and have fun; so that's what we did that spring.
Ernie:	And all summer.
Caroline:	Yeah, well we started about it casual but we ended up engaged. We started dating in April and we got engaged in July. Now he had orders to go back to Key West and I didn't know what I was supposed to do. Should I sign my contract for another year? Should I go to Key West and teach school, or ... What should I do? Anyway, we got engaged in July and we got married in September. I figured if I was going to make a go of this as a new mom I would have to cut out my teaching and that was the hardest thing for me to do because I loved it. The youngest one was just going into kindergarten, so he was only in school half a day. Anyway, Marilyn and Warren dated too. Warren says to Marilyn one day, "Well if Ernie Plantz can do it, I guess I can too. Let's get married." They got married in February.
Ernie:	Yep. He ended up making Admiral.
Caroline:	They went all over the world.
Ernie:	He was a commodore over in Korea.
Caroline:	And he was the CO of *Kamehameha* out in Hawaii.
Ernie:	Right. CO of the Kamehameha, the submarine.

Caroline:	At first Ernie wouldn't let me meet the kids. I finally said to him, "If I can't get along with them, this marriage is a no-go. That's quite important." Well, Marilyn got to meet her future kids. Caroline didn't get to meet hers because he didn't want to upset them. Marilyn was invited to a picnic that Caroline wasn't invited to.
Ernie:	But the kids went.
Caroline:	The kids were at the picnic.
Ernie:	Yeah.
Caroline:	But I wasn't invited to the picnic...
Ernie:	I know that.
Caroline:	...because he didn't want to upset them.
Ernie:	Right.
Caroline:	I called Marilyn and I said well how was it, and she said it was great. I said did you meet Ernie's kids? Oh yeah. I said well tell me about Billy's ears. He was the youngest. She said "Billy's ear? What about Billy's ears?" Ernie had told me that he was okay but his ears were on upside down, and backwards, and it was only a problem when it rained. I was so gullible that I believed him. She just cracked up laughing. She said his ears are fine and they are mounted on the right way. I should have known then what I was getting into!
Ernie:	Well I warned you.
Steve:	Can you tell me about all of your children? I've heard about all of them I think, but I never got your children's names in order.
Caroline:	They do have names.
Steve:	Now is the oldest Linda?
Caroline:	Yes. Nancy's the next one. Then William and Elizabeth and David. I inherited the first three the day I got married. Then we had Elizabeth and David and from one who said he wasn't going to have any more kids. He wasn't very sympathetic though. I remember I wanted a bassinet for baby Beth and he said, "No, I'll just clean out one of my dresser drawers; she can sleep

Plantz Family – Ernie's 90th Birthday:
(L to R) Back – Beth and Tessa, Nancy, Beth K. and William, Linda, David and Jack.
Front – Caroline, Hattie, Ernie and Jesse.

there." She was born in '67 and David was in '76. The other wives on the *Bushnell* helped. Yes. I loved getting on the *Bushnell* because the Captain always called me "The Bride."

Ernie: I had lots of good people that pulled me out of a hole when I started to sink, I think.

Caroline: Yes. Good people.

Laurels and Recognition

Steve: What kind of awards or medals did you receive?

Caroline: Steve, take a look at this nomination packet I made up for the Connecticut Veterans Hall of Fame.

Steve:	Oh yes. That makes it easy. That's an impressive list. Some of the more notable are:
	Bronze Star
	Purple Heart
	POW Service Medal
	Good Conduct Medal with six stars.
	Of course, your dolphins and war patrol pin with star.
	Inducted with the first class into the Connecticut Veteran's Hall of Fame
	The Good Conduct Medal though; are you sure about that?
Caroline:	Good one!
Ernie:	Well, it's important not to get completely caught. Or at least to have a friendly hand to get you out of scrapes; I had both.
Steve:	Yes, just kidding a little. That's truly an impressive collection and one you should be proud of.
Ernie:	Well, some I liked and some I didn't. I was never one to crow about me and my doings. Very few in the Navy knew I was a prisoner, former prisoner, because I didn't tell them. I wanted to make my own way on my own efforts. I didn't want any sympathy. When us *Perch* boys would get together some might talk about something funny that happened in the camp but mostly I just kept it to myself.

CHAPTER 14

LIVING WITH SURVIVAL

Reunions and the return of the Perch

Robison and Ernie at a Perch reunion, c. 1985

Ernie:	I was the youngest onboard all the others were older than me.
Caroline:	And that's how you got the nickname, "The Kid".
Ernie:	Right.
Caroline:	We went to a reunion. At that point our youngest daughter was maybe three or four. She was the type of

child, you could tell her no, and no meant no. You know, we only had to say it one time. So when we walked into this reunion, and I'm holding her hand, the men there said, "There's *The Kid*!" I'm thinking; what did she do? You know, what happened that I missed; did she misbehave? Come to find out, this was *The Kid*. But I hadn't known it until then.

Ernie: I was he.

Caroline: I found out. One of the wives there also told me when we were first married, she said, "I have to get you aside and tell you. The bond that these guys have is closer than any other bond; husband, child, wife. There's nothing quite like the bond that they have." She said, "I just want you to know as you start off in this family, you might not like it, but that's the way it is." She was right and understandably so.

Steve: That kind of exceptional experience must create a connection deeper even than family or friends or children.

Ernie: Yes.

Caroline: Now tell him what happened at Thanksgiving in '06. What did they find?

Ernie: What was found? Oh, the old *Perch*.

Steve: Your boat?

Ernie: Yeah, the Australian divers were looking for a British cruiser, the *Exeter* that had gone down in the same battle. They were using sonar, side-scan sonar. And they spotted this long, you know, cylinder shape lying on the bottom and they thought it was interesting enough that they would go down to see what it was. Lo and behold, that's what they saw; it was the *Perch*. This picture was in the paper. See this marker on the side? When EB built it, they put a builder's plaque on the fairwater, outside the Conning Tower. It says, what it is, USS *Perch*, submarine. That's my boat.

Perch's (SS-176) plaque photographed by Kevin Denlay,
December 2006.
*Courtesy of Charles R. Hinman, Director of Education &
Outreach, USS Bowfin Submarine Museum & Park*

Ernie: The guy in charge of the *Bowfin* museum out in
           Hawaii, that museum out there, he contacted me and
           I kept the secret until they were ready to announce it
           to the world. He swore me to it but wanted us old
           Perch men to know right away. Good guy; quite a
           Thanksgiving for me.

Escaping from a Different Kind of Prison

Post-traumatic stress disorder (PTSD) is a mental health condition that's triggered by a terrifying event — either experiencing it or
witnessing it. Symptoms may include flashbacks, nightmares and
severe anxiety, as well as uncontrollable thoughts about the event.[1]

Steve:	Now I understand that you had a difficult time overcoming the experiences of the prison camp.
Ernie:	Yes. Yes I did. You understand that there were some things that happened in the camp, seemed almost every day, that were just horrible. I have mentioned some of them but you don't want to hear them all and I don't want to tell them.
Steve:	I can see that. You didn't talk about it when you were in the Navy either.
Caroline:	And you felt, so you said, like you hadn't done your part.
Ernie:	I was a little bit ashamed of how I spent the war because a lot of my shipmates died and I lived. I thought that I lived because I helped the Japs. They died because they were fighting the Japs. That's enough to make you feel guilty. Very guilty.
Caroline:	But it wasn't a choice you had. It was a choice that was forced on you.
Ernie:	Well, that's true.
Steve:	Did you continue to have difficulty coping even after you got out of the Navy?
Ernie:	I would have to say yes.
Steve:	In what way?
Caroline:	Well, you never told anybody that you were a POW.
Ernie:	No, ah, ah. I didn't do that. I didn't want people to feel sorry for me, or I wanted to make it on my own, and I did really. I just kept mum about my previous experience.
Steve:	Was that the only effect?
Ernie:	I think it affected my outlook on life. In particular, you begin to think about the possibility of dying since you got your friends all around you and they are dying.
Steve:	Right.
Ernie:	I don't know. It made me a bit more aware of your surroundings, and your life, and your connections.

Steve:	How about anything else like problems sleeping or nightmares?
Ernie:	Initially I had nightmares but they subsided fairly early.
Caroline:	But then they came back when you used to be fighting in bed, remember?
Ernie:	I remember.
Caroline:	That's when you moved down the hall because you were afraid you were going to break my nose or something even though I put a pillow between us. All because you thought you were still fighting the Japanese.
Ernie:	I did a lot of fighting the Japanese in my mind; those were bad, bad scenes.
Caroline:	Do you remember Linda's birthday? When she turned twenty-one?
Ernie:	Yes.
Caroline:	I wanted to know what great thing we were going to do for her special day. Ernie looked at me with this very serious face and said "Do you know where I was when I turned twenty-one?" and that was the end of the discussion about what great thing we were going to do.
Ernie:	I did say that. I feel bad about that. She didn't deserve it.
Caroline:	Well you would never talk about the war or any of your experiences so they didn't understand. The kids knew that he'd been in the war but they didn't know anything about what he had done or what had been done to him.
Ernie:	I didn't think they wanted to hear that mess and I didn't want to have to think about it.
Caroline:	Now I don't know how many years ago it was but we started going to a PTSD group that met down in West Haven. That really helped a lot. I wish they had that group fifty years ago; Post Traumatic Stress. While

attending these sessions Ernie started talking freely about it which was different and I have to believe so healthy because he never talked about it all the time that the kids were growing up. I mean they knew he was a POW but they didn't know any of the specifics at all. And really, the whole experience influenced a lot of the way he interacted with his family and with others.

Ernie: I would have to say that's true.

Caroline: But that group was a blessing. Once he started talking it was like it was relieving some sort of old pressure inside.

Ernie: Maybe it was like that old coconut wound; it looked healed but it wasn't really healed; we had to open it up again.

Steve: That's a great analogy.

Caroline: But it wasn't until the mid-1990s that we started going to the meetings. Every Thursday morning we would be down there for the PTSD group and Ernie was the only submariner. Most of them were Army and they'd been in the march, the Bataan Death March.

Ernie: In fact I was the only submarine sailor there in the group.

Caroline: The wives, we had our own little clique, and the guys were there with Mrs. Hill who was a facilitator. Each time I'd drive home, he'd open up a little bit more. Now, you get him talking about the war and it used to be that I'd have to say "Okay Ernie, stop, that's enough for right now." It really has affected parts of his life I think.

Steve: After you went through with that VA group that was at West Haven how did that make you feel? Did you feel better afterwards? More relieved?

Ernie: I think in the long run I did, yeah. In the short term I uncovered things that I had tried to hide. It makes you sad and a bit unhappy. In the long term I think it was good for me because I got a lot of stuff off of my heart that I couldn't have done any other way.

Steve: I think a lot of people don't realize that with any of the talking therapy you feel worse at first. You've kept it in that room and now you are going to open that door and you're like "Oh, there it all is." Maybe it helps dissipate it, I don't know.

Ernie: There are two sides to it; you have got to open that door but at the same time you've got to continue on with your life and not dwell on it.

Steve: Right.

Ernie: Not focus only on what comes through that door.

Steve: Right.

Ernie: It's a past pain and it's not right now. Nobody can change that. I thought it was probably good to talk about it. Yeah, but don't make a lifetime of it. Some guys that were in that circumstance never did anything but talk about that and that wasn't really good either. You didn't make a career of it. You did do what you needed to do. There are a lot of guys that were like that.

Steve: Right, I think that the door behind which you keep all of that bad stuff, I think keeping it closed all the time is bad. Keeping it open all the time is bad too.

Caroline: There has to be a happy medium.

Steve: I believe you've got to have control over it. I think that, just from what I've heard, that's what groups like this help you do. They help you be able to control it. You learn how to open it a little bit and how to get it back shut. You don't have to lean against that door as much as time in the therapy goes on.

Caroline: You're absolutely right. Yeah, I think it was very worthwhile. It was a good thing.

Ernie: Yeah, it was a good thing for me. I don't know if it would be good for everybody, but it certainly was good for me. Different people think differently. What fits one doesn't necessarily fit another. That's a big mistake we make in thinking that everybody thinks alike, because they surely don't.

145

Steve: I think you're right. I don't know if that's just an American trait but we seem to always think that when something new comes along we think that this is the one thing that'll fix it. Really solving problems most often takes many things.

Caroline: Correct.

Ernie: It's an American trait I think to be optimistic. Consequently, bad things happen, they try to hide it. That's behind me, I've done that, been there. They may have done that and been there, but it's not over.

Steve: Excellent.

Returning to the Camp

Ernie: You know, after a while I felt good enough that I made some plans. I wanted to see old Doc Borstlap and I did in 1993.

Steve: You got to see the doctor that saved your life?

Ernie: I did. I went to Holland for a reunion over there with a Dutch-American friend and we looked up the doctor who was still living. I had lunch with him and talked for a couple of hours.

Steve: Oh, that's great.

Ernie: Yup. And here we are. Good old Doc. I asked him about, you know, what he had done to me when I was unconscious. I knew what I had heard and I told him what I knew. He said "I remember the case but I didn't do just exactly what you tell me." I said "What's the real story?" He said, "Well, it is true that I crushed quinine tablets but I didn't mix them with tap water; I mixed the powder with fermented coconut juice. Then I gave you an injection with a homemade needle. The juice seemed the most sterile liquid available" I said to him "You SOB, that explains a lot to me!" He said "What do you mean boy?" Imagine us talking this way; I'm in my late

146

Doctor Borstlap and Ernie, c. 1993

seventies and he's in his eighties. "What do you mean boy?" I replied "That's probably why I've been a drinker these last fifty years!" He says, "You jest!" and we laughed and laughed. What a good, good man. Thank God for Doc Borstlap.

Steve: How great that you could meet with him after all that time and after all you had been through together.

Ernie: Yes it was. I saw him once again when I went back to the old camp. Paid a visit and spent two weeks out there. I always I wanted to go back.

Steve: You went back to the prison camp in Makassar?

Ernie: That's right. It was in 1997. I couldn't get any of the crew members to go with me. So my Dutch-Indonesian friend was going, he was trying to go by flying west to get there and I was flying east to Singapore by myself. I got myself a hotel room because I got there before he did; he showed up a day later. And then we

	flew on to Indonesia together and stayed in the hotel room together. Things had changed a lot.
Steve:	I'm sorry, who was this friend?
Ernie:	Oh. There was this half Dutch, half Indonesian guy named Rob, Rob Walters, that lived in the house where the prisoners used to go by on the way to the working parties. When the war was over he went to Holland and took an aviation mechanic course and then he got a job in Dutch Aviation in New York. He was living out on Long Island. I don't know how he heard about me, but he...
Caroline:	I think it was someone at EB that told him about you.
Ernie:	Yeah. His buddy from Holland, a refugee, was working at EB, and the both of them visited me here from time to time. Funny but that's how I met him, through this guy at EB. We were in the same place but I never knew him during the war. Maybe I saw him, maybe not.
Caroline:	We used to see a lot of him afterwards.
Ernie:	Yes. He had a cousin that was living in The Hague so I went with him one time and we stayed at his house. I was there for a week or so; about two weeks I was gone, I think. They helped me locate the Doc.
Caroline:	He knew the language so that made it easy when he took you back where the camp was.
Ernie:	That's right.
Steve:	Okay. Now I don't imagine any parts of the camp were still there.
Ernie:	The first camp we were in was still there. There was still the old hospital but they had turned it into a modern Indonesian hospital. They'd added an extra wing to it but I could still recognize it. It was still there. But the Japs had had us build a circular outside fish tank out of used brick.
Steve:	Oh yeah. Like a fish pond?
Ernie:	Yes and darned it if that thing wasn't still there after all those years. But there had been a big mango tree in the yard and that was gone, but the stump was there.

148

Rob Walters at Former Japanese Military Hospital, 1997

Entrance to the Original Dutch Camp, 1997

Steve:	What was that like going back there? Difficult for you?
Ernie:	Difficult in a way, I guess, but it freed me up a little bit. The Indonesians were good to me. I'm a member of the Lion's Club so I contacted a Lion's Club in Makassar and they held a special day for me. I remember that it was on Easter Sunday. We went to a combination family picnic and visit to an Indonesian country school. They had bought supplies for me to pass out to the school kids and so they had the kids all lined up in school uniforms, boy, squeaky-clean. So we passed out, oh, pencils and paper, reading material and then took pictures. After we went back to a wide place near a rice paddy where they'd set up a picnic spot. They had their families there and they'd brought food from home and they'd hired Indonesian fishermen; the rice paddy was flooded and it had fish in it. He'd catch a fresh fish and he grilled it right there in front of us. Also there were these great big old prawns; they were like big shrimp. He had a whole bunch of those things. When we started eating well as fast as I'd eat one big prawn, why the wife of the Indonesian local politician would have two more peeled on my plate. So we had a good day.
Steve:	That sounds great! What hospitality!
Ernie:	The next day I had to leave so they took me to the airport which was about twenty miles away which was nice.
Steve:	So Rob was a big help getting around?
Ernie:	Yes. Somehow Rob was like one of us. He would go to all the Perch reunions.
Steve:	Was he your age or younger?
Caroline:	He was younger.
Ernie:	He was a boy, really - a teenager - when we were there as prisoners. And then when the war was over, then he immigrated to Holland. We befriended him but I

think the war destroyed all of his connections to his home. He was a man without a country.

Caroline: That's right. But he did go to all the *Perch* reunions so he had you guys. He died alone and nobody quite knows what happened. He used to go back to Indonesia all the time to check on his relatives or if somebody had died and so forth. But he died quite a few years ago.

Ernie: Rob was always worried about his mother and father. They were buried on the island, back on Celebes, and it seems he tried to go back every year, to check on their graves. Finally, he got so sick I guess he couldn't go. Next thing I knew, he was dead.

Caroline: Nobody knew what happened.

Ernie: He wasn't that old of a man; he was probably at least ten years younger than me.

Caroline: We don't know where he was buried or anything. Nobody could ever find out. He never married. He was an interesting person. You had some good trips over yonder with him.

Ernie: Yes. I never knew his whole story but I feel like he was a casualty of the war too. His wounds just took a longer time to kill him.

Chapter 14 Notes:

1. Information from http://www.mayoclinic.org/diseases-conditions/post-traumatic-stress-disorder/basics/definition/con-20022540 [accessed 4/10/2015]

CHAPTER 15

ONE OF THE LAST *PERCH* BOYS

Home, family, and friends

Steve: Now who is this young fellow?

Ernie:	That's me!
Caroline:	Oh Ernie!
Ernie:	That's my friend Captain Paul McHale's son Ben McHale at his Eagle Scout Ceremony. That was in April of last year.
Caroline:	April 12, 2014.
Ernie:	Right. I always liked to do things for the community so when they asked me to be a part of this I said yes.
Caroline:	You worked on the Zoning Board too.
Ernie:	And I was the chairman.
Steve:	Was that here in Ledyard.
Ernie:	Yes. I was on the Ledyard Zoning Board for, oh, ten years I'd say and four of those as chairman. And I have always been very active with the Lions. I've also enjoyed being with my friends at SubVets WWII. It's been a great organization and a great bunch of guys.
	Here I am when I returned from a Freedom Flight to Washington, D. C. Oh it was about 2010. Most of my whole family was there to meet me when I returned so maybe they caught my happy surprise in the picture. Yeah; that was nice.

Steve:	Great picture.
Caroline:	Ernie became a Lion's Melvin Jones fellow.
Steve:	What is that?
Caroline:	It is the organization's recognition of a member's dedication to humanitarian service; I'm quoting from the citation.
Steve:	That's a wonderful recognition.
Ernie:	It was but I don't need the big awards. I made it out of that camp when a lot of times I thought I wasn't going to. Maybe that made me want to do things for others who were in bad situations. I don't know. I know I'm pretty grateful. The only thing is when I was unconscious Jesus told me that I was going to live; I didn't think he meant forever! I'm starting to wonder when he is coming for me.
Caroline:	Oh Ernie!
Steve:	Yes, don't be in a rush. There are people who still need and want you to be here. You continue to influence lots of people like young Ben McHale who's in the Naval Academy now.
Ernie:	Well that's nice to hear and that may be but I've had a long life and a good one. I've raised hell certainly but I don't think I've gone out of my way to hurt anyone. Death has been around me several times but never taken me. I've had a lot of good people care about me and a good Lord who's watched over me. Though I've been through some awful times I have been given quite a lot of good things actually. I hope I've given back as much.

Ernie and Caroline, 2012

SELECTED BIBLIOGRAPHY

Primary Sources

Books

Jane's Fighting Ships of WW II. London: Studio Editions Ltd., 1989. Originally published by Jane's Publishing Co. 1946/47.

Military Publications

United States Navy. *The Fleet Type Submarine – NAVPERS 16160*. Washington: US Government Printing Office, 1946, reprint by www.periscopefilm.com.

The Bluejackets' Manual. Tenth Edition. Annapolis, Maryland, United States Naval Institute, 1940.

United States Submarine Losses – World War II. Washington: U. S. Government Printing Office, 1946. Revised and reissued as NAVPERS 15,784 in 1949.

Interviews by the Author

Plantz, Ernie, Chief Electrician's Mate / Lieutenant, USN. Interview by author, 26 June 2009, Ledyard, Connecticut. Digital recording – transcribed.

Plantz, Ernie, Chief Electrician's Mate / Lieutenant, USN. Interview by author, March through October, 2015, Ledyard, Connecticut. Digital recording – transcribed.

War Patrol Reports

Arnette, E. H., F1c, USN. USS *Perch* (SS 176), "Statement after War Patrol Number One and liberation from POW camp." 12 October 1945.

Crist, Daniel, EM3c, USN. USS *Perch* (SS 176), "Statement after War Patrol Number One and liberation from POW camp." 12 October 1945.

Hurt, D. A., commanding, "USS *Perch* (SS 176), Report of War Patrol Number One". Commander Submarine Force Pacific Fleet, 17 January 1942, typewritten and library bound; Book 176, U. S. Navy Submarine Force Museum, Groton, Connecticut.

Hurt, D. A., commanding, USS *Perch* (SS 176), "Statement after War Patrol Number One and liberation from POW camp." 12 October 1945

Secondary Sources

Books

Bagnasco, Erminio, ed. *Submarines of World War Two.* Annapolis, Maryland, Naval Institute Press, 1977.

Barnes, Robert Hatfield. *United States Submarines.* New Haven, Connecticut: H. F. Morse, 1946.

Blair, Clay Jr. *Silent Victory: The U. S. Submarine War Against Japan.* New York: J. B. Lippincott, 1975.

Christley, Jim. *U.S. Submarines 1941-45.* Oxford, UK: Osprey Publishing, 2006.

Hargis, Robert. *U.S. Submarine Crewman 1941-45*. Oxford, UK: Osprey Publishing, 2003.

Hoyt, Edwin P. *Submarines At War: The History of the American Silent Service*. Brancliff Manor, NY: Stein and Day, 1983.

Parrish, Thomas. *The Submarine: A History*. New York: Viking/Penguin, 2004.

Roscoe, Theodore. *United States Submarine Operations in World War II*. Annapolis, Maryland: United States Naval Institute, 1949.

Zim, Herbert S. *Submarines: The Story of Undersea Boats*. New York: Harcourt, Brace and Co., 1942.

INDEX

CPSIA information can be obtained at www.ICGtesting.com
Printed in the USA
BVOW02s1409311215

431434BV00003B/212/P